Recent Extinctions

Carsten R. Jorgensen

Written and published in Canada.

ISBN: 0-9949338-7-8
ISBN-13: 978-0-9949338-7-4

DEDICATION

To all the animals on the brink of extinction and to all those
working tirelessly to save them.

CONTENTS

ACKNOWLEDGMENTS

All images in this book are known or thought to be public domain or permission has been granted by the owners or are under creative commons licenses.

Thank you to the following Pixabay.com contributors who graciously provided many of the wonderful photos and images for this book:

Blickwinkler
Kees Koertshuis
Roland Winkelmann
Raik Thorstad
Nick115
Fxxu
Tracy Angus-Hammond
e-smile
Ssmiling
MrsBrown
Musthaq Nazeer
Ирина Гиязова
Mohamed Nuzrath
Public Domain Pictures
Ronbd
Christoph
skeeze
Heather Griesbach

Cover Design by Dana Woodard
with the use of images from
Open Clip Art Vectors
Artsy Bee
jplenio
from Pixabay.com

Thank you to Cory Hughes for the idea for this book

1 EXTINCTION EVENTS

Extinctions have occurred continuously since life began on the planet Earth. Charles Darwin's 'Origin of Species' describes that species change very slowly as time progresses. With time, species develop new characteristics and the individuals with the new characteristics, which are beneficial in the environment in which they live, go on to survive. Others go extinct. With time, some individuals with new characteristics develop into new species. In the past, old species became extinct and new species developed and survived.

Extinctions came about gradually and new species developed gradually. However, sometimes the environment changed drastically so that there were mass extinctions.

Paleontologists recognize five mass extinction events. In these five extinction events more than 75% of the animals disappeared.

The first occurred at the end of the Ordovician period; about 444 million years ago. Jaime Murcia, of the Museum of Victoria, stated that 86% of the animal species became extinct. Most of the animals lost were Graptolites. These sea creatures were filter feeders and colony builders. The individuals were about 2 to 3 cm in length.

Melbourne Museum paleontologist, Rolf Schmidt, has stated that this mass extinction was probably caused by climate change. It is thought that the duration of the event took place over one million years and was caused by a short, severe, ice age. This came about because of the uplift of the Appalachians which exposed silicate rock that sucked carbon dioxide out of the atmosphere and chilled the planet. The resulting ice age caused sea levels to drop and killed off the Graptolites.

The second mass extinction came in the late Devonian period; 375 million years ago. Seventy five percent of Earth's species were lost. Chip Clark, of the Smithsonian Institution, stated that it was probably caused by the newly formed land plants that had grown to cover the earth. It is believed that their roots, which penetrated the soil, stirred up the earth releasing nutrients into the ocean. This triggered algal blooms which sucked oxygen out of the water. Bottom dwellers then died of lack of oxygen.

A great many of the bottom dwelling species were trilobites. 550 million years ago, during the Cambrian period, Trilobites appeared to become the most diverse and abundant animal. There were many species of trilobites. These animals had survived the first extinction event but were now wiped out in the Devonian extinction event.

A trilobite fossil

The third mass extinction event is known as 'The Great Dying' and 96% of the animal species went extinct. This event occurred at the end of the Permian age, 251 million years ago, and nearly ended life on earth. Jaime Murcia, of the Melbourne Museum, stated that the Tabulate corals were lost in this event and that today's corals are an entirely different group. The cause is thought to be a volcanic eruption near Siberia which hurled vast amounts of carbon dioxide into the atmosphere. Methagenic bacteria belched out methane, a greenhouse gas, causing global temperatures to rise. The oceans then became acidic and released poisonous hydrogen sulphide.

The fourth mass extinction event occurred 200 million years ago at the end of the Triassic Period. In this event, 80% of the species were lost. This event was enigmatic for the paleontologists. No one has been able to determine the cause. One interesting discovery from the Triassic Period was the fossil conodont.

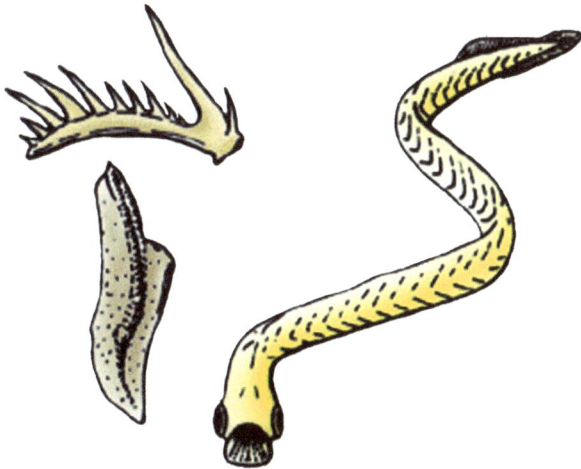

Two conodont teeth (left) and a conodont (right). The teeth are greatly enlarged. The size of conodonts varied from 0.03 mm to 3 mm in length.
Illustration by Philippe Janvier, 1997 - Tree of Life Web Project, CC BY 3.0, https://commons.wikimedia.org/w/index.php?curid=22921782

Paul Taylor, of the Natural History Museum, stated that the conodont had small teeth built from hydroxyapatite, a calcium rich mineral which is a key component in our own teeth and bones today.

The fifth mass extinction event took place 66 million years ago. This ended the Triassic period, wiping out the dinosaurs. This was caused by an asteroid hitting the Yucatan Peninsula in Mexico. It threw debris into the atmosphere which blotted out the sunlight for years. This caused the extinction of 76% of all species. This ended the Cretaceous Era and was the start of the Cenozoic Era.

2 THE SIXTH MASS EXTINCTION EVENT

Scientists have claimed that we are now in the sixth mass extinction event. They have stated that humanity has wiped out 60% of mammals, birds, and reptiles since 1970 and that this is now an emergency that threatens civilization.

Some scientists have stated that we are not yet in the sixth mass extinction event. However, these scientists state that we are on the verge of the sixth event.

Bygone generations of Europeans and people originating from Europe looked to Genesis in the Bible and had concluded that man's purpose was to subdue and tame the earth. This caused man to look on nature as a separate entity to be used for exploitation and commerce. By clearing land, draining swamps, introducing foreign species into habitats, damming rivers, and hunting, humans have made vast changes to nature.

Biologists became alarmed. They stated that our existence depends on the natural world. In 1968, biologist Garrett Hardin published an article entitled "The Tragedy of The Commons". It explained that a resource that belonged to everyone which was exploited would go extinct unless some control was exercised. This article was one of many that influenced people to take on a different view of the animal species in nature. People became conservation minded.

Another publication that influenced people to become conservation minded was the book 'Silent Spring' by Rachel Carson published in 1962.

The following chapters contain descriptions of some animals that have recently become extinct.

3 WOOLLY MAMMOTH

**Woolly Mammoth -
The tusks grew to about 8 feet in length.
Females had no tusks**

About 27 to 30 million years ago, the ancestor of the mammoth appeared in North and South America. The mammoth was similar in size to the modern elephant. But they had much smaller ears and foreheads. They were covered with a coat of thick brown hair which grew to a length of 35 inches. The woolly mammoth weighed from 4 to 6 tons and the modern elephant weighs from 3 to 7 tons. Woolly mammoths were from 8 to 10 feet from foot to shoulder. The modern elephant is from 5 to 12 feet from foot to shoulder.

With time, the woolly mammoth spread to all the continents except for Antarctica and Australia. Their main habitat was spruce woodlands around valleys and swamps. It is believed that the woolly mammoth was hunted to extinction after the last ice age.

An isolated population of woolly mammoths existed on St. Paul Island until 5,600 years ago. Another population existed on Wrangel Island, an island in the Arctic Ocean, between the Chukchi Sea and East Siberian Sea, until 4,000 years ago. The woolly mammoth was declared extinct in 1796.

In 1799, the first fully documented woolly mammoth skeleton was discovered. In 1806, it was brought to the Zoological Institute of the Russian Academy of Science. It was there that Wilhelm Gottlieb Tilesius put the pieces together. He based the positioning of the bones by comparing them to that of an Indian elephant skeleton. Tilesius was successful in reconstructing the first skeleton of an extinct animal except for one error. He had put the tusks in the wrong sockets, so that they curved outward instead of inward.

4 IRISH ELK

Irish Elk

Contrary to it's name, the Irish Elk was not an elk at all but was, in fact, a deer. This was the largest known deer that had ever lived. It was 7 feet tall at the shoulders and weighed about 1500 pounds. The antlers could reach 144 inches from tip to tip and weighed up to 88 pounds.

Since a great number of good quality skeletons of this animal have been found in Irish bogs, it became known as the Irish Elk. It first appeared about 400,000 years ago. Other finds were made in Europe, North Africa, China, and Russia.

Many scientists think that the Irish Elk suffered from starvation during the recent ice age which ended 11,600 years ago and thus went extinct. However, fossils of the Irish Elk found in Russia have been dated to approximately 7,000 to 8,000 years ago which was a period of warm climate.

It would seem that the Irish Elk did not become extinct due to starvation and their massive antlers were adequate protection from predators. It is very likely that the Irish Elk were hunted by humans to extinction.

5 DODO

Skeleton cast and model of dodo at the Oxford University Museum of Natural History, based on modern research
(Photo by FunkMonk - licensed under the Creative Commons Attribution 2.0 Generic   https://commons.wikimedia.org/w/index.php?curid=20054563)

The Dodo's closest relative was called Rodrigues solitaire, which is also extinct. They both belonged to the family of pigeons and doves.

The Dodo bird lived on the island Mauritius, east of Madagascar, in the Indian Ocean. In the dense forests of the island lived many types of birds, but there were no mammals on the island. The Dodo had no predators. The Dodo was flightless, weighed up to 50 pounds, and lived and nested on the ground. It ate the fruits that fell from the trees.

A ship from Portugal came to the island in 1505. These Portuguese were the first humans to set foot on the island. After that, the island became a regular stopover for ships engaged in the spice trade. The dodo then became a source of meat for sailors. A great number of Dodo birds were killed for food.

In 1598, a Dutch squadron under Admiral Nishal Teeluck landed at Grand Port and named the island Mauritius. In 1638 the Dutch inhabited the island. They exploited ebony trees. They also introduced sugar cane and domestic animals. Their domestic animals included deer and monkeys. Rats escaped from the ships and started to inhabit the island.

The rats, pigs, and monkeys ate all the Dodo eggs on the ground and the humans ate the Dodo birds. The last Dodo was killed in 1681. At this time, the Dodo was just one of the large numbers of bird species driven to extinction on Mauritius.

In the 19th century the dense forests were cut down so that tea and sugar plantations could be established. This caused many more birds to become extinct. There were 45 bird species on the island when it was discovered. Only 21 species managed to survive.

An individual species in nature is always a part of the ecology of its habitat. A scientist recently noticed that a certain species of tree, the Calvaria, or Tambalacoque tree, was becoming quite rare. The trees were about 300 years old. The lifespan of this species of tree is 300 years. They would soon all die and become extinct. The Dodo bird had become extinct 300 years ago. Was there a connection?

Yes. The Dodo ate the fruit of this tree. It was only by passing through the digestive tract of the Dodo that this tree's seeds could become active and grow. This tree species would now become extinct.

Some creative scientists did some experiments to try to keep these trees from disappearing from the planet. They discovered that domestic turkey gullets were sufficient in mimicking the Dodo bird's digestive system. They used turkeys to begin a new generation of the tree. There is now hope that these trees will be saved and survive. The tree has been named 'the Dodo tree'.

A Dodo Tree (otherwise known as a Calvaria, or a Tambalacoque tree)

6 STELLER'S SEA COW

A family of Steller's Sea Cows (1889)

The German naturalist, George Steller, was part of an expedition led by the Danish explorer, Vitus Bering. In June 1741, the expedition set sail from Kamchatka in two ships. A few weeks later they reached Alaska. Bering permitted Steller to search for new species but allowed him only a single day. Steller managed to describe several new species of bird. One of these was Steller's Jay. At the beginning of winter, the two ships became separated. Two landing parties vanished and most of the expedition members had scurvy.

In November, the ship that George Steller was on, ran aground on an island. The men thought that it was part of the Russian mainland. But Steller soon realized that it was an island. Stellar foraged for herbs which overcame his scurvy. The island had foxes that followed him. They snatched his food and implements. George realized that these bold foxes had never seen humans before.

One day, while walking along the beach searching for firewood, George saw a huge black shape moving about in the shallows. It looked like an overturned boat. Every once in a while a snout would emerge from the water and draw a breath. This was the first sighting of a Sea Cow.

Steller was amazed to see that this was a type of manatee. The sea cow was about 30 feet long and weighed close to 10 tons. A single sea cow could feed the entire shipwrecked men for a month.

When word got around about how much food the sea cow could provide, men went out and hunted them. In 1768, less than 30 years after they were discovered, the Steller Sea Cow was extinct.

Recently ecologists have developed an alternate theory of how Steller's Sea Cow became extinct. The Sea Cow was an obligate algivore. It ate nothing but sea weed (mostly kelp). Sea urchins also eat sea weed. The sea otter ate sea urchins. The Aleutians and Russians over harvested the sea otters. This caused a population explosion of sea urchins which ate all the algae. Thus the Sea Cow went extinct due to starvation.

In all likelihood, it could very well have been a combination of both theories; over hunting and starvation.

7 RODRIGUEZ GIANT TORTOISES

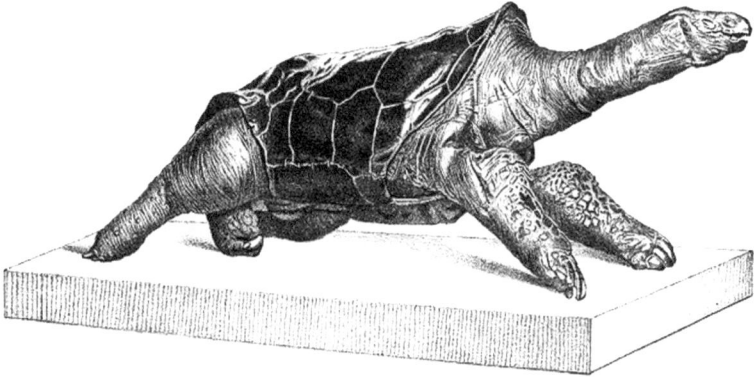

The Saddle-backed Rodriguez Giant Tortoise

There were two types of tortoise found on the island of Rodriques in the Indian Ocean; the saddle-backed giant tortoise and the domed giant tortoise. This island has an area of 42 square miles. The island was found in February 1548 by the Portuguese explorer Diogo Rodriques. The island was uninhabited. It had unique endemic plants and animals. One of these was the Rodriques giant tortoise.

The saddle-backed Rodriques giant tortoise had a thin light shell with unusual large apertures which enabled the tortoise to have greater mobility for the elongated legs and neck. It could browse leaves as high as four feet off the ground. It shared Rodrigues Island with its much smaller relative, the domed Rodriques giant tortoise.

The domed Rodrigues tortoise was one of the smallest of the giant tortoises of the Indian Ocean. Where the saddle-backed Rodriques giant tortoise was a high grazer, the domed Rodrigues tortoise was a low grazer of grasses.

Both species were descended from an ancestral species, which colonized Rodrigues by sea many millions of years ago, and then differentiated into the two Rodrigues species. At the time of the arrival of human settlers, dense tortoise herds of many thousands were reported on Rodrigues.

In 1601, the Dutch began visiting the island more often. The tortoises on the island were now hunted as fresh food and living ballast. The turtles could live a long time without food and water so they could be used as fresh meat. Then ships would not have to carry salted meat. There were so many loaded onto ships at a time and the shells of the tortoises were so thin that many of them were crushed to death. This hunting of the Rodriques giant tortoise drove it into extinction by 1802.

As late as 1802, there is mention of survivors reportedly being killed in the large fires used to clear the island's vegetation for agriculture, but it is not clear which of the two Rodrigues species these were, and which survived the longest.

It was discovered that the Rodriques giant tortoise was essential to the ecosystem of the island. One of its roles was in the regeneration of the island's forests.

In an attempt to restore the balance of this ecosystem the people of Rodriguez introduced a replacement giant tortoise. They introduced the radiated tortoise of Madagascar. The radiated tortoise is closer in appearance to the domed Rodrigues tortoise than the saddle-backed Rodrigues tortoise.

The Radiated Tortoise
Photo By Charles J Sharp - Sharp Photography
https://commons.wikimedia.org/w/index.php?curid=75120298

The radiated tortoise is an endangered species because of habitat destruction and poaching.

8 GREAT AUK

Great Auk

(Photo by Mike Pennington, CC BY-SA 2.0)
https://commons.wikimedia.org/w/index.php?curid=13812423

The Great Auk was a small flightless bird about 27 inches tall and weighed about 10 pounds. They were comparable to antarctic penguins in their gait. They walked about the same speed as a man. Their short wings had a white trailing edge and there was a large white patch in front of each eye.

The Great Auk lived on scattered offshore islands in the North Atlantic. They lived on islands off Canada, Greenland, Iceland, The British Isles, and Scandinavia. When not on these islands for breeding, they were foraging on the open ocean where they ate small fish.

These birds were monogamous. The female laid a single egg and it took 44 days of incubation to hatch. The male and female took turns to do the incubation. The hatchling developed rapidly and became a fledgling in 9 days. After this, the family left to forage in the ocean. It took seven years for a fledgling to become mature.

The Great Auk ate small fish: menhaden, shad, 3 spined sticklebacks, white sea bass, and flatfish.

The Great Auk did not show fear when approached by man. It became hunted for food and its oil. Sailors would walk up to the nests, kill adults and young and take the eggs.

On July 3, 1844, a hunter named Sigurdur Isleifsson strangled the last two adults while his partner, Ketill Ketilsson smashed the egg the birds had been incubating with his boot.

The Great Auk once numbered in the millions. They were hunted to extinction.

9 HARELIP SUCKER

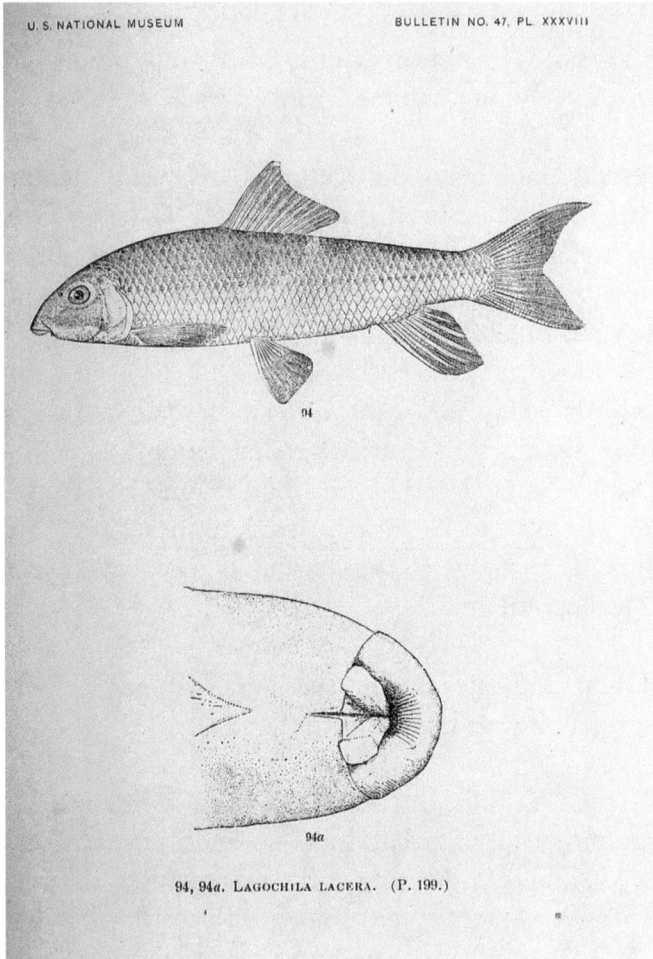

U. S. NATIONAL MUSEUM   BULLETIN NO. 47, PL. XXXVIII

94

94a

94, 94a. LAGOCHILA LACERA. (P. 199.)

Harelip Sucker Fish

Very little is known about the Harelip Sucker fish. It was found in rushing fresh water streams in south eastern United States. The harelip sucker was only 7 inches long. The first specimen was caught in 1859. It was described by biologists 20 years later when it was nearly extinct. It went extinct because of siltation of its clear water stream habitat.

10 ATLAS BEAR

The Atlas Bear

The Atlas bear was the only bear native to Africa. This bear lived in the Atlas mountains and the surrounding areas of Morocco, Algeria and Libya. The bear had shaggy, blackish brown, hair 4 to 5 inches long. The muzzle was black. It had an orange rufous chest and belly. The bear ate mostly roots, acorns, and nuts.

After Rome defeated Carthage, it established the province of Africa (North Africa) in 146 BC. The Roman Empire eventually controlled the entire Mediterranean coast of Africa.

The Romans hunted the atlas bears. They caught them live and took them back to Rome. In their arenas they would bring in animals to be hunted to the cheering crowds of the spectators. Animals hunted in the arenas included rabbits, deer, lions, tigers, crocodiles, and Atlas bears.

The more carnivorous and large animals were also used to execute criminals and, for a while, Christians. The Atlas bear was one of the animals used to execute criminals. The crowds cheered. Atlas bears (as well as lions and tigers) were also sometimes used in events with gladiators.

The Romans wiped out most of the Atlas bears. However, a few bears survived. The last Atlas bears to be seen were killed by hunters in the 1870s.

11 KAWEKAWEAU

Artists rendition of the Kawekaweau

In New Zealand, Maori tradition stated that large lizards lived in the dense forests. They were reported from widespread localities from the northern half of North Island. It was reported as being an arboreal (tree climbing) lizard about two feet long. It was the largest known species of gecko.

By 1871 it had become very scarce. F. E. Manning and Hokianga obtained two live ones. One of them was devoured by a cat. The other one escaped.

In 1873 an Urewara chief killed a kawekaweau which was found under the loose bark of a rata near Whakatane. He described it as "two feet long and as thick as a man's wrist; colour brown, striped longitudinally with dull red."

There were no more sightings. There were now doubts that the kawekaweau had ever existed.

In 1979, Alain Delcourt, a curator of the Museum d'Histoire Naturelle in Marseille, France, discovered an unusual specimen in the Museum's zoological collections. It was thought to be a gecko over two feet long.

Alain sent pictures to the United States hoping for a positive identification. Aaron Baur and Tony Russel, specialists in gecko taxonomy, determined that the Marseille specimen belonged to a group of geckos found only in New Zealand, New Caledonia, and the Eastern seaboard of Australia. They became certain that the specimen belonged to a Genus found only in New Zealand and was in fact the lost "kawekaweau", the giant forest lizard of Maori oral tradition. The stuffed gecko went to the National Museum in Wellington in 1990.

12 QUAGGA

Quagga

The quagga was a variety of plains zebra found in South Africa. Because of their beautiful hides, they were highly prized by hunters. They also competed for grazing with livestock, so they were hunted to extinction by hunters and farmers. By the 1870s they were gone from the wild.

On August 12, 1883, the last captive quagga, a mare, died in the Amsterdam Zoo. Its death was not recognized as signifying the extinction of its kind at that time, and the zoo requested another specimen; hunters believed it could still be found "closer to the interior" in the Cape Colony. It was officially declared extinct in 1886; three years after the last one had died.

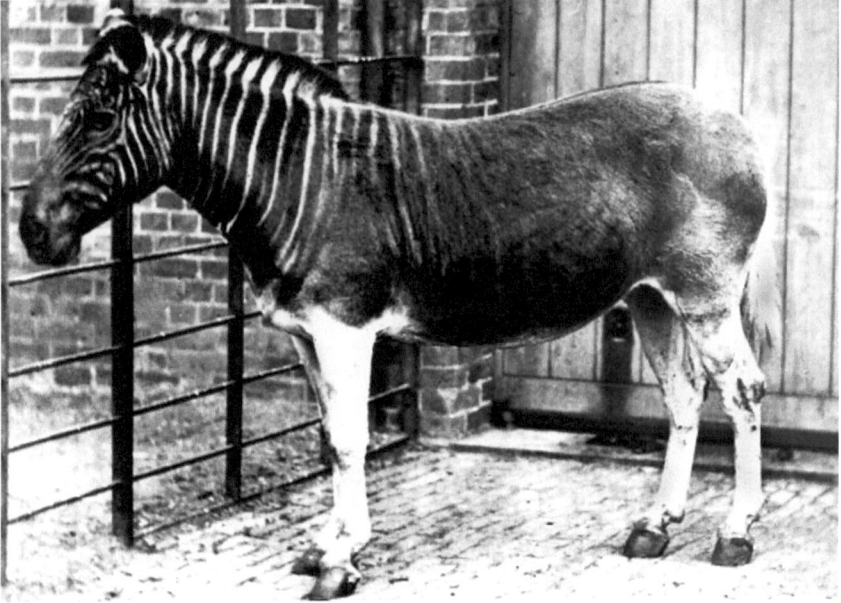

Quagga mare at the London Zoo in 1870.
(The only specimen ever photographed alive. Five photographs of this specimen are known to exist, taken between 1863 and 1870).

In 1984, the quagga was the first extinct animal to have its DNA analyzed. This study launched the field of ancient DNA analysis.

After the very close relationship between the quagga and plains zebras was discovered, Reinhold Rau started the Quagga Project in 1987, in South Africa to create a quagga-like zebra population by selectively breeding for a reduced stripe pattern from plains zebra stock. The eventual aim is to introduce them into the quagga's former range. These quaggas are referred to as "Rau quaggas". The founding population consisted of 19 individuals from Namibia and South Africa. They were chosen because they had reduced striping on the rear body and legs. The first foal of the project was born in 1988. Once a sufficiently quagga-like population has been created, participants in the project plan to release them in the Western

Cape. This type of selective breeding is called "breeding back". The practice is controversial, since the resulting quaggas will resemble the original quaggas only in external appearance, but will be genetically different. The technology to use recovered DNA for cloning does not yet exist.

**Regular plains zebras and Quagga Project zebras
in Mokala National Park**
(Photo by Bernard Dupont CC BY-SA 2.0
https://en.wikipedia.org/wiki/Quagga_Project)

13 SEA MINK

The American mink is closely related to the sea mink and has the same colouring but is smaller in size.

In the early days of the fur trade, unusually large mink fur came out of Halifax. The sea mink was the largest mink found. It was bigger than the Alaskan mink. It was a marine mammal but stayed close to the shore line. It lived along the rocky coasts and islands of New England and the southern maritime provinces of Canada. It was found in the Bay of Fundy and the Strait of Belle Isle. It was described as being larger than a fox.

It was prized for its fur and was hunted so rapidly that it became extinct in the late 1800s. The last two recorded kills of a sea mink were made in Maine in 1880 near Jonesport, Maine, and Campobello Island, New Brunswick in 1894. However, the 1894 kill is speculated to be that of a large American mink. Fur traders made traps to catch sea minks and also pursued them with dogs, although they were rarely trapped. If a sea mink escaped into a small hole on the rocky ledges, it was dug out by hunters using shovels and crowbars. If it were out of reach of the hunters, it was shot and then retrieved using an iron rod with a screw on the far end. If it were hiding, it was smoked out and suffocated. The minks' nocturnal behavior may have been caused by pressure from fur traders who hunted them in daylight.

To add to the problem of over-hunting, the sea mink had a very high infant mortality rate, which meant they could not reproduce fast enough to keep up their population.

14 PASSENGER PIGEON

The Passenger Pigeon

Before the 1800s, there were billions of passenger pigeons in North America. These pigeons migrated in huge flocks. When a flock of passenger pigeons flew into an area, they darkened the sky. During some migrations, the flocks flying overhead would stretch for over a mile and could take several hours to pass. The American ornithologist, John James Audubon described a huge flock of passenger pigeon as a storm.

When such a flock nested, there were great disturbances. There were breaking of branches due to overcrowding. The huge deposits of guano choked out vegetation by covering it up.

The huge flocks ate seeds and insects. When these birds nested in huge flocks, predators found meals easy to obtain. The piles of guano created a rich community of decomposers which lasted months after the birds had migrated on. Sunlight reached the forest floor because of the canopy thinning. This enabled thick under story vegetation to grow. The plants growing there attracted pollinators and herbivores. Reptiles and amphibians flourished in the warm sunlight and there was abundant insect life and bird densities. The dense vegetation provided cover for small mammals.

As the forest regenerated, the canopy closed again causing a community shift. Roosting sites were created for bats, owls, squirrels, woodpeckers, and many other species. Patches of mature oaks and chestnuts provided seed crops for many species of foragers. These seed crops also enticed the passenger pigeons to come back and start the cycle all over again. The passenger pigeon dispersed seeds all over North America.

The passenger pigeon was like a storm creating successional habitats all over the eastern North America. They fostered a higher level of biodiversity and bioproductivity than any single homogeneous habitat is capable of doing.

The passenger pigeon provided a food source for the indigenous people of North America. Because of such huge low flying flocks, birds could be killed by throwing sticks at them. Sometimes, they were taken by nets. Up to 800 could be taken at a time. When North America was colonized, the colonists also hunted and ate passenger pigeons.

Soon there was a move afoot to declare the passenger pigeon as a pest. Farmers were killing passenger pigeons to try to save their crops from these huge flocks of seed eating birds.

In 1703, the Bishop of Quebec excommunicated the passenger pigeon. Basically, this meant that the passenger pigeon had committed a grave spiritual offense that caused it to be spiritually separated from the Church and the community of the faithful. Thus, the passenger pigeon was deprived of all sacraments.

The passenger pigeon would now be allowed to go to Mass but not to receive the Holy Eucharist. These heretical birds were now also deprived of a Catholic burial.

In the 1800s the hunting of passenger pigeons greatly increased. In 1896, the last flock of 250,000 birds was slaughtered by hunters. These hunters knew that this was the last flock left.

Martha, the last known passenger pigeon, died in captivity in Cincinnati, Ohio, on September 1, 1914. She was 29 years old.

Martha, the last known passenger pigeon

15 YELLOWFIN CUT THROAT TROUT

The Yellowfin Cut-Throat Trout

The yellowfin cut-throat trout was described by scientists in the 1891 Bulletin of the United States Fish Commission. This fish reached a weight of 10 pounds and it had bright yellow fins. The fish was found in Twin Lakes, in the state of Colorado.

Anglers decided that a more active fish would be great for the Twin Lakes. Rainbow trout were then stocked. The rainbows interbred with the cut-throat. The cut-throat became hybridized with the rainbow and bred out of existence. The last yellowfin cut-throat trout disappeared in 1903.

16 CAROLINA PARAKEET

**Mounted specimen of the Carolina parakeet in the
Museum Wiesbaden, Wiesbaden, Germany.**
(Photo by Fritz Geller-Grimm, CC BY-SA 2.5
https://commons.wikimedia.org/wiki/Conuropsis_carolinensis#/media/File:Karo
linasittich_01.jpg)

The Carolina parakeet had beautiful coloured feathers. It had red and yellow on its head. This was the only parakeet found in North America. It was common from the Ohio Valley south to the Gulf of Mexico.

It became fashionable for women to wear Carolina parakeet feathers in their hats. This fashion caused the Carolina parakeet to be hunted to extinction. The last known wild Carolina parakeet was killed in Okeechobee county, Florida in 1904. The last Carolina parakeet, a male named Incas, died in the Cincinnati Zoo on February 21, 1918.

17 BUBAL HARTEBEEST

The Bubal Hartebeest
Photographed by Lewis Medland in 1895

The Bubal Hartebeest was once very common in North Africa and the Middle East. European hunters came and hunted them for sport and meat. After the French conquest of Algeria, entire herds were massacred at once by the colonial military. Hunting is what wiped out the Bubal Hartebeest. The last captive Bubal Hartebeest died in the Paris Zoo in 1923. The last wild Bubal Hartebeest was shot in Morocco in 1925.

There are other subspecies that currently live in grasslands south of the Sahara. The red hartebeest and Lichtenstein's hartebeest, are considered subspecies of the common hartebeest, and are present in southern Africa.

18 CASCADE FUNNEL-WEB SPIDER

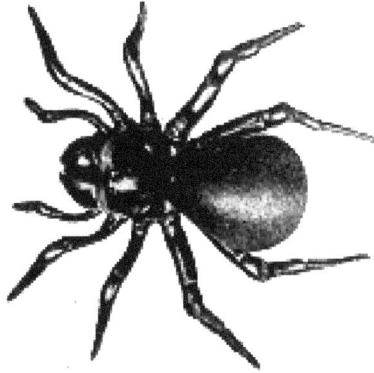

Drawing Of The Cascade Funnel-Web Spider by Hickman – 1926

The cascade funnel-web spider was described by the biologist Hickman in 1926. He had found two spider burrows in soft soil near the bank of a creek in the Cascades area near Hobart, Tasmania. One burrow was 18 cm deep with a silken tube inside. The tube contained an egg capsule.

The place where the spider was found was destroyed by urbanization. There are no other records of this spider. It is now listed as extinct.

A Female Funnel-Web Spider
(No photos of the Cascade Funnel-Web spider exist. This is a
close relative to the Cascade Funnel-Web Spider)

19 SILVER TROUT

The Silver Trout

The silver trout was found in only three small lakes in New Hampshire. In the deep waters of these lakes, cut off from the other species, the silver trout had no natural predators.

Then, these lakes were stocked with recreational fish. Yellow perch, which eat trout eggs, and lake trout, which eat and hybridize with other char species, were particularly devastating. The stocked fish out competed the silver trout so that it went extinct. The last silver trout were caught in 1930.

20 HEATH HEN

The Heath Hen

The Heath hen was a sub species of the Greater prairie-chicken. They lived in the scrubby heath land barrens of coastal North America from southernmost New Hampshire to northern Virginia.

The Heath hen was so easy to hunt and favoured for food that by 1870 there were no more Heath hens on the main land. There were about 300 left on the island called Martha's Vineyard off Massachusetts. By 1890, there were only 120 – 200 birds left. The decline was caused by feral cats and poaching.

In 1927 there were only twelve and two were female. By the end of the year there were 5 males left. This was in spite of the best protection which could be used at that time. On December 28, 1928, only one Heath hen was left. He became known as Booming Ben. He was last seen on March 11, 1932.

Heath hens were one of the first bird species that Americans tried to save from extinction. A bill "for the preservation of heath-hen and other game" was introduced in the New York State legislature in 1791. Although the legislation was passed, it turned out to be unenforceable.

Although the effort to save the Heath hen from extinction was ultimately unsuccessful, it paved the way for conservation of other species.

21 SRI LANKA SHRUB FROG

Sharp-snouted Shrub Frog

There is not very much information on many frogs that have gone extinct.

Sri Lanka has lost over 17 species of shrub frogs to extinction. However, 2 of those shrub frogs have been rediscovered; the Spotted Shrub Frog in 2009 and the Webless Shrub Frog in 2010. The rediscoveries were thanks to researchers who found them in a part of the Peak Wilderness Sanctuary that had never been explored by scientists. Although they were discovered in a protected area, they are still listed as critically endangered.

Perhaps with more exploration they may even discover some shrub frogs that are still listed as extinct such as those listed here:

Gunther's Shrub Frog
Striped-snout Shrub Frog
Farnland Shrub Frog
Leopard Shrub Frog
Sharp-snouted Shrub Frog
Pointed-snouted Shrub Frog
Southern Shrub Frog
Malcolm Smith's Shrub Frog
Maia Shrub Frog
White-nosed Shrub Frog
Pattipola Shrub Frog
Blunt-snouted Shrub Frog
Queenwood Shrub Frog
Dimbulla Shrub Frog
Thwaite's Shrub Frog

It is thought that the Sri Lanka shrub frogs went extinct because of urbanization and possibly a disease.

It appears to be largely a result of the loss of 95 % of the island's perhumid forests. Research on Sri Lanka's amphibian extinctions have been aided by studying the specimens collected in the period 1850–1940 and preserved in overseas natural-history museums.

The Sri Lanka Petite Shrub Frog is listed as endangered

Photo by Buddhika.jm(Buddhika Mawella) - Own work, CC BY-SA 4.0
https://commons.wikimedia.org/w/index.php?curid=61489809

Some species of the Sri Lanka Shrub Frog still exist but remain at imminent risk.

22 TOOLACHE WALLABY

The Toolache Wallaby

The Toolache wallaby was a small kangaroo. It was 2.75 feet long and was slim and graceful. It was considered to be the most beautiful of the kangaroo species. They were very social animals and lived in groups.

A combination of things caused the decline and eventual extinction of the Toolache wallaby. One of the larger factors was the destruction of its habitat. The preferred habitat of the Toolache Wallaby was a dense, tall sedgeland and grass community that developed on the clay soils of plains between dune ridges. Once the swamps were drained and cleared out by human settlers, much of the wallaby's habitat was destroyed too.

The introduction of predators such as the European Fox were another factor in the decline of the Toolache wallaby population.

The other main factor was that the Toolache wallaby was hunted for its beautiful fur and for sport. Hunters often used greyhounds to run it down.

The last wild sighting was thought to be in 1924. A remnant population was then discovered in the 1930s. An attempt was made to capture some for breeding in captivity. Ten out of fourteen were killed in attempting to capture them. The remaining four eventually died of exhaustion and shock.

The last known Toolache wallaby survived for 12 years in captivity. It was a female with a joey in its pouch. They died in 1939.

23 XERCES BLUE BUTTERFLY

Xerces Blue Butterflies
Photo by Brianwray26 - Own work, CC BY-SA 4.0,
https://commons.wikimedia.org/w/index.php?curid=36453811

The Xerces blue butterfly was first described in 1852. It was of great interest to butterfly fanciers. The individual Xerces blue butterflies had incredible variations in their wing patterns.

This blue butterfly was native to the sand dunes of coastal San Francisco. It became extinct due to loss of habitat, in particular the Lotus plant which it fed on, due to urbanization.

The last Xerces blue was seen between 1941 and 1943.

24 MASTODON

Life reconstruction of American Mastodons
By Charles R. Knight , 1896

Mastodon first appeared in the early Miocene period 27 to 30 million years ago. They were smaller than the woolly mammoth and the elephant.

Compared to mammoths, mastodons had shorter legs, a longer body and were more heavily muscled; a build similar to that of the current Asian elephants.

Mastodon on the right and Wooly Mammoth on the left
By Dantheman9758 at the English Wikipedia, CC BY-SA 3.0,
https://commons.wikimedia.org/w/index.php?curid=4289640

Their ears were smaller, and they were shorter than the elephant. Their bodies were covered with reddish brown hair. They are thought to have been contemporary with North American native groups of people.

Mastodons appear to have fed upon leaves. They had a distinctive characteristic of the grinding teeth in that they are low-crowned, large, and strongly rooted, with as many as four prominent ridges separated by deep troughs. The prominent upper tusks were long and grew parallel to each other with an upward curvature. Short lower tusks were present in males but absent in females.

Mastodon Molars at the State Museum of Pennsylvania

The mastodon began to disappear about 10,000 years ago. The reason was thought to be human hunting.

In the 1960s while I was studying biology at Queen's University in Kingston Ontario, one of my biology professors informed the class that, in a certain valley in Africa, there were found a few herds of mastodon in the 1950s. They were exterminated by ivory hunters.

25 GRAVENCHE

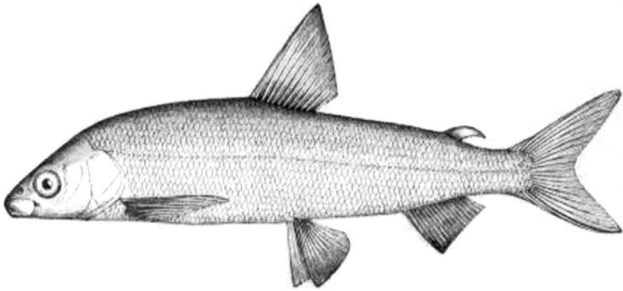

The Gravenche

The gravenche was also known as the Lake Geneva whitefish. The gravenche was a foot long relative of the salmon.

The gravenche became over fished. In the early 1920s it had disappeared. The last gravenche was seen in 1950. There are no gravenche specimens anywhere.

25 THICKTAIL CHUB

The Thicktail Chub

The thicktail chub lived in California's Central Valley. It's habitat was marshes, lowlands and weed choked back waters. The backs of the thicktail chub ranged in color from greenish brown to purplish black. The sides and belly were yellow. This fish was minnow sized.

In 1900, it was the most common fish in Sacramento Valley and San Francisco Bay. California's native population used it as a food fish.

As the San Francisco settlement grew it became over fished by commercial fishermen. The thicktail chub's habitat was converted into farm lands. Most of its habitat was destroyed by the drainage of sloughs and marshes, dam-building, and water diversion for irrigation. All this resulted in the loss of the sluggish water the species preferred.

The last sighting of this fish was on April 13, 1957.

27 LAKE TITICACA ORESTIAS

The Lake Titicaca Orestias

The Lake Titicaca orestias grew to a maximum length of 11 inches.

Lake Titicaca is a small lake in South America lying on the border between Peru and Bolivia. The government controlling the lake wanted to improve tourism. The government introduced exotic fish to improve angling. Lake trout were introduced in 1936. Rainbow trout were introduced in 1942 and silverside were introduced in the 1950s.

The silverside were observed eating orestias. It is very likely that the lake trout and rainbow trout also ate orestias. By 1960 the Lake Titicaca orestias were extinct. The only two Lake Titicaca orestias left today are preserved specimens in the Natural Museum of Natural History in the Netherlands.

28 TECOPA PUPFISH

The Tecopa Pupfish

The Tecopa Pupfish lived in the hot springs of California's Mojave Desert. It lived in water with a temperature of about 110 degrees F.

In the 1950s and 1960s bath houses were built in the hot springs vicinity. The hot springs were then enlarged and diverted. The resulting swifter currents caused downstream water temperatures to rise above a level to which the pupfish were adapted.

These modifications also allowed the Amargosa River pupfish, which are related to the Tecopa Pupfish, to migrate upstream from the Amargosa River and hybridize with the Tecopa pupfish.

These factors caused the extinction of the pupfish. The last pupfish was caught in 1970.

29 LAKE PEDDER EARTHWORM

Earthworm similar to Lake Pedder earthworm (no photos exist of the Lake Pedder earthworm)

The Lake Pedder earthworm was discovered in Tasmania in 1971. It was lacking dorsal pores and was semi-aquatic. The Lake Pedder earthworm was a species of segmented earthworm with 129 body segments. The head and back had faint brown colouring and the clitellum (the smooth, short section of skin that secretes cocoons) was pinkish and buff. It has been described from a single, slightly damaged, specimen observed in 1971 and there are no known photographs.

This earthworm became extinct in 1972 when Lake Pedder was deliberately flooded for the building of a hydroelectric facility.

30 ROUND ISLAND BURROWING BOA

The Round Island Burrowing Boa (1880)

The Round Island burrowing boa was found on the small islands around Mauritius. It was found most often in the topsoil layers of volcanic slopes.

Its population had dwindled by the 1940s. After 1949, it could be found only on Round Island. Humans had introduced non-native species of rabbits and goats to the islands. The rabbits and goats destroyed the vegetation and upset the habitat of the boa. The Round Island burrowing boa was last seen in 1975.

31 MADEIRAN LARGE WHITE BUTTERFLY

The Madeiran Large White Butterfly

The Madeiran large white butterfly was endemic to Madeira. Its natural habitat was the laurisilva, or laurel forest. It was last seen in 1977. A fifteen-year survey was conducted in the 1970s and 1980s to try to find them. It was never found. The Madeiran large white butterfly is now thought to be extinct.

In the 1950s, the small white butterfly was introduced to Madeira. These butterflies were later found to be carrying a virus. It is now thought that this virus wiped out the Madeiran large white butterfly.

32 YUNNAN LAKE NEWT

The Yunnan Lake Newt

The Yunnan Lake newt was found only near the Kunming Lake in Yunnan province, China. There it lived in the shallow waters of the lake and nearby water habitats. It went extinct in 1979 because of pollution, loss of habitat, and introduced species.

33 GALAPAGOS DAMSEL

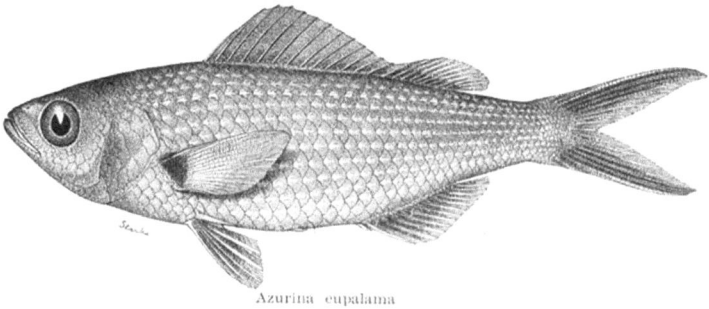

Azurina eupalama

The Galapagos Damsel

The Galapagos damsel, also known as the blackspot chromis, was olive-gray with a blue tinge, and silvery along the sides. It had a black spot at the base of each pectoral fin. It had a prominent lateral line.

The Galapagos damsel was a plankton eater. In the 1980s there was a temporary increase of water temperature around the Galapagos islands caused by the El Nino currents. This killed the local plankton causing the damsel to become extinct.

34 GASTRIC BROODING FROG

The Gastric Brooding Frog
Photo by unknown. Used under "fair use" for purposes of fact.
https://en.wikipedia.org/wiki/Gastric-brooding_frog

The gastric brooding frog was a ground dwelling amphibian in Eastern Australia. It had an unusual method of reproducing. After the eggs were fertilized by the male, the female would take the eggs into her mouth and swallow them. The eggs would hatch in the stomach and the young would stay there. During the time the eggs were in her stomach the female would not eat.

When the young emerged from the mother's mouth, they were fully formed frogs. The emergence took place over a long time. Sometimes as long as a week. Up to 25 small young frogs would be regurgitated. If the mother was disturbed, she would regurgitate her brood in a sudden propulsive vomiting.

The gastric brooding frog was infected with an amphibian disease. This caused its extinction. The last sighting of this frog was in 1981. In August 2010, the Amphibian Specialist Group of the International Union for the Conservation of Nature organized a search for the frog. None were found.

The Gastric Brooding Frog giving birth through its mouth.

Photo: Australian Government Department of the Environment, Water, Heritage and the Arts

35 TASMANIAN TIGER

The Tasmanian Tiger (Thylacine)

The Tasmanian tiger was not a tiger. It looked like a dog. But it was not a dog. This animal was a carnivorous marsupial. It was the largest carnivorous marsupial of modern times. The thylacine was one of only two marsupials to have a pouch on both the male and the female. The other is the water opossum. The Tasmanian tiger was relatively shy and nocturnal.

Farmers were afraid that the tigers were killing their sheep. Therefore, a bounty was placed on the animal which caused intensive hunting for the tigers. After intensive hunting for 100 years, the tiger was declared extinct in the 1930s. Wilf Batty, a farmer, killed the last Tasmanian tiger. He saw it patrolling outside his house so, he went out and shot it.

The Tasmanian tiger held the status of endangered species until the 1980s. At the time, international standards were that an animal could not be declared extinct until 50 years had passed without a confirmed record. Since no one had ever provided definitive proof of its existence in the wild for more than 50 years, it met that official criterion. Tasmanian tigers were declared extinct by the International Union for Conservation of Nature in 1982 and by the Tasmanian government in 1986.

Despite being declared extinct, the Australian Rare Fauna Research Association reports having 3,800 sightings on file from mainland Australia since their extinction date. There have been photos and even films taken of them but, unfortunately, none of these were clear enough to be considered actual proof of their existence. So, their status currently remains as "extinct" but there is the possibility that they could still exist. The search for them continues.

36 BLUE WALLEYE

The yellow walleye or pickerel (top), The blue walleye or pickerel (bottom)
Photo contributed by Gary of Walleye Heaven

The blue walleye, also called the "blue pike" (but was not a pike at all), was endemic to the Great Lakes of North America.

Morphometric studies led biologists to classify the blue walleye as a separate species in 1926. Listed as an endangered species by the United States in 1967, it was declared extinct in 1983 due to over fishing.

However, people have still been catching blue coloured walleye since the 1983 declaration of extinction. Why is this?

Genetic analyses conducted in 2014 show that the blue walleye was not genetically different from the yellow walleye, but was a unique color morph of the yellow walleye, rendering the taxon blue walleye invalid.

Dr. Wayne Schaefer says that the "Blue walleye of Canada are genetically different than the extinct "blue pike" of Lake Erie. They are albino for yellow color and have blue color in the mucous of their skin. The blue color forms on the dorsal (upper) part of the body and is particularly noticeable in the two dorsal fins and the upper part of the tail. "

The extinct "blue pike" differed from today's blue walleye in that it had a steel blue-grey colour, larger eyes that were located higher on the head, and a smaller interorbital distance. It's range was restricted to Lake Erie and Lake Ontario.

Some blue walleye have been caught with a blue mucus on it's skin. The blue mucus is a pigment protein, named "sandercyanin". Little is known about the source of the protein or it's function, but the University of Wisconsin Milwaukee - Washington County is currently doing research on blue walleye and sandercyanin in Canada and the upper Midwest. Studies show that sandercyanin concentrations were significantly higher in fish collected in the summer versus other seasons. It is thought that it could be like a type of sunscreen for fish. Some people believe that is what makes the blue colour of the fish. However, yellow and blue walleyes in the study did not differ in amounts of sandercyanin. So, it is most likely not what makes today's blue walleye a blue colour.

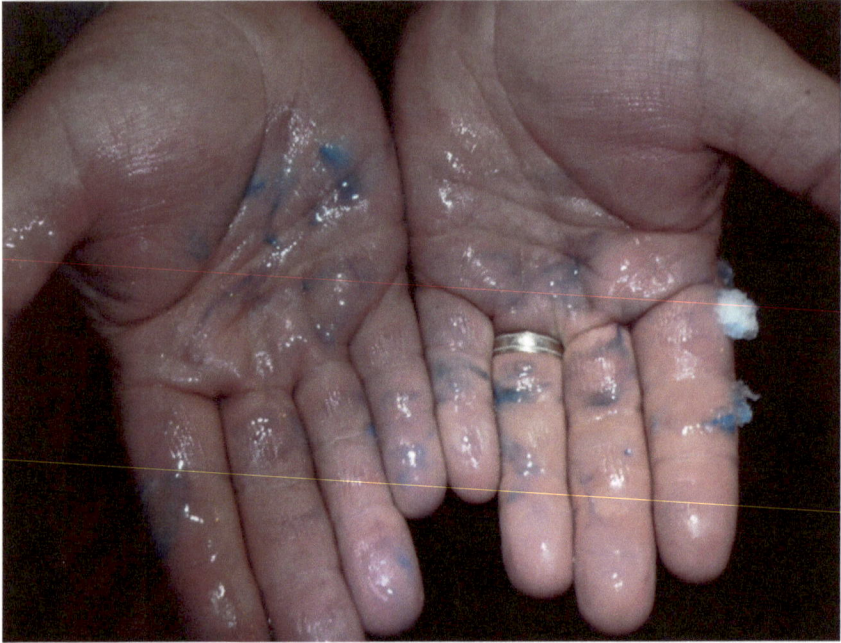

Blue sandercyanin comes off in your hands after handling a fish coated with it.
Photo contributed by Gary of Walleye Heaven

Gary hosts a website where people have sent in pictures of the blue walleye that they have caught:

https://www.walleyeheaven.com/blue-walleye.htm

On his website he talks about catching blue walleye that had blue meat. The question arose as to why the meat was blue. This might be explained by noting where the sandercyanin is produced in the body of the walleye. Sandercyanin is produced in membrane-bounded vesicles just towards the back of each dorsal spine and next to an adjacent blood vessel. It is possible that the blue colour somehow enters the blood stream and travels through the body creating the blue coloured meat; much like that of a white flower turning blue when you add blue food colouring to its water. Sandercyanin does not affect the health of the fish, nor does it affect the taste of the meat.

There have been times when extinct species have been rediscovered in small pockets of the world. Perhaps, with enough searching, we may be lucky enough to rediscover a small population of the extinct "blue pike" hiding in plain sight among our blue walleye one day.

37 GOLDEN TOAD

A male Golden Toad
Photo by Charles H. Smith

Many small animals have gone extinct without any one noticing. The golden toad would have been one of them except for its golden colour. The males were a brilliant orange colour. The females looked different, but just as spectacular. The females were slightly larger than the males, and were dark olive to black with spots of scarlet encircled by yellow.

The golden toad was first seen in the cloud forest of Costa Rica in 1964. Since then it has been seldom seen. The last documented sighting was in 1989.

The golden toad is now thought to be extinct. The cause was originally thought to be due to a severe neotropical drought in 1987-1988, but other factors have since been treated as more likely causes such as climate change, a fungal infection, or both.

38 LEVUANA MOTH

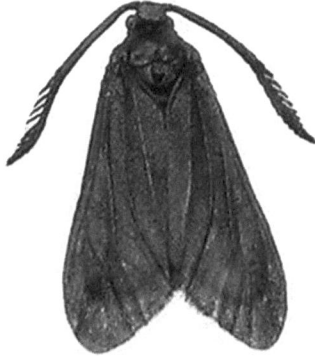

The Levuana Moth

The Levuana moth was a day-flying insect with a wing span of 16 mm. The head and thorax was steely blue. The abdomen and legs were an ochre colour. They lived on Fiji Island.

In 1877 an outbreak of Levuana moths became a serious pest. They devastated coconut plants. Coconut cultivation became unprofitable. The moth was devastating coconut plantations and nearby wild trees.

In 1916 the moth started to expand its range. Cultural and chemical controls failed to work on the moth. In 1925, John Douglas Tothill introduced a biological control by using a general parasite which greatly reduced the Levuana moth populations. It eventually caused the extinction of the Levuana moth. It has been considered extinct since 1994.

Since the Levuana moth prefers to feed on the tallest coconut palms in highly localized areas, it is possible that they still exist, undetected, in very small numbers. It is believed that if they do still exist, they are inhabiting the neighboring islands of Fiji.

39 PYRENEAN IBEX

The Pyrenean Ibex

The Pyrenean ibex was very abundant in the Pyrenees Region.   During the nineteenth and twentieth century the Pyrenean ibex was forced to share its habitat with sheep, domestic goats, cattle, and horses.   This led to inter specific competition and over grazing.   The ibex had the additional disadvantage of being hunted by humans.

In the second half of the twentieth century there was only a small population left. This population was found in the Ordesa National Park in the Spanish Central Pyrenees.

The last Pyrenean ibex was found dead on January 6, 2000. A tree had fallen on her.

40 CASPIAN TIGER

The Caspian Tiger

The Caspian tiger was also called the Hyrcanian tiger, Turanian tiger, Babre Mazandaran tiger, and Persian tiger depending on the habitat in which it was found.

The Russian colonization of Turkestan during the last half of the nineteenth century began the demise of the Caspian tiger. Tigers were killed by large parties of sports men and military personnel who also hunted the tiger's prey, the wild pig.

The range of wild pigs declined drastically between the middle of the nineteenth century and the 1930s. This was caused by over hunting, natural disasters, and diseases including swine fever and hoof and mouth disease. This caused large rapid die offs.

Two Caspian Tigers

The extensive reed beds of tiger habitat were converted to crop land for planting cotton and other crops. During the twentieth century, the regular Russian army was used to clear predators from forests, around settlements, and potential agricultural land. About 100 tigers were killed each year in the forests of Amu Darya and Piandj rivers.

The final wild Caspian tiger is said to have been killed in February 1970, in Hakkari Province, Turkey. It was declared officially extinct by the IUCN in 2003.

41 CARIBBEAN MONK SEAL

The Caribbean Monk Seal

The Caribbean monk seal was the only seal native to the Caribbean.

Like other monk seals, this species had a distinctive head and face. The head was rounded with an extended broad muzzle. The face had relatively large wide-spaced eyes, upward opening nostrils, and fairly big whisker pads with long light-colored and smooth whiskers. Caribbean monk seals were also known to have algae growing on their pelage, giving them a slightly greenish appearance.

Its lack of fear of humans and an unaggressive and curious nature was taken advantage of by human hunters and it was hunted to extinction. The main reason for hunting was to obtain the oil held within their blubber which was used for things like oiling machinery.

Another factor was the over fishing of the reefs. With little to feed on, the seals that were not killed by hunters did not have enough to survive on and either starved or did not reproduce.

The last confirmed sighting of a Caribbean Monk Seal was in 1952 at Serranilla Bank, between Jamaica and Nicaragua. It was declared extinct in 2008.

A Caribbean Monk Seal in the New York Aquarium in 1910

42 WESTERN BLACK RHINOCEROS

The Black Rhinoceros

Photo: Hans Stieglitz
License information: Creative Commons Attribution CC BY-SA 3.0,
https://de.wikipedia.org/wiki/Datei:Schwarzes_Nashorn-01.jpg

The western black rhinoceros, or West African black rhinoceros, were found in Angola, Kenya, Mozambique, Manibia, South Africa, the United Republic of Tanzania, Zimbabwe, Ethiopia, Cameroon, Chad, Rwanda, Botswana, Malawi, Swaziland, and Zambia.

They were a subspecies of the black rhinoceros and were genetically different than other rhinoceros. They were browsers, eating leafy plants and shoots. They were near-sighted and depended on the local flocks of birds to warn them of approaching danger.

The black rhinos were heavily hunted at the beginning of the twentieth century. One reason for this was that rhino horns were believed to have the power to cure certain ailments. It was also used to make ceremonial knife handles. One kilogram of horn cost more than $50,000.

For much of the 1900s it was estimated that there were 850,000 western black rhinoceros. Widespread poaching between 1970 and 1992 brought the population down to about 2,500 in 1995. Rhinoceros poaching continued. It was estimated that there were only 10 western black rhinoceros left in 2000. In 2001 there were only 5 left.

The last sighting of the western black rhinoceros was in Cameroon's northern province in 2006. The western black rhinoceros was declared officially extinct in 2011

43 CAPE VERDE GIANT SKINK

The Cape Verde Giant Skink by
J. Terrier - Rochebrune, A.-T. (1885)

The Cape Verde giant skink was large for a skink. It could grow to a length of 13 inches from the snout to the vent and the tail would equal this length, making it 26 inches from the snout to the tip of its tail.

This skink lived on the islets of Branco and Raso in the Cape Verde islands in the Atlantic Ocean. It was a herbivore and was also partly arboreal.

When the Cape Verde islands were made bare of vegetation by humans and domesticated animals, centuries ago, the Cape Verde skink adapted to the resulting semi-desert conditions. Then, despite being a herbivore, it would occasionally eat young resting shore birds.

The Cape Verde giant skink became over hunted for food. At one time, starving convicts were marooned on the Cape Verde Archipelago and became resident skink hunters. It was also hunted by the natives of neighbouring islands for skink oil. In 2013, the Cape Verde giant skink was declared extinct.

44 RABB'S FRINGE-LIMBED TREE FROG

The Rabb's Fringe-Limbed Tree Frog

Photo: Brian Gratwicke
License information: Creative Commons Attribution CC BY 2.0,
https://commons.wikimedia.org/w/index.php?curid=18339583

The fringe-limbed tree frogs lived in the forest canopy of Central Panama. They were a relatively large frog. When descending from the trees, they could glide by spreading the webbing of their enormous hands and feet.

The fringe-limbed frog males were territorial and guarded the water filled tree holes used for breeding. The males also guarded the young and supplied them with food. It was the only known frog where the young tadpoles obtained their nutrients by feeding on the skin cells of their father.

The frog was first discovered in 2005. In 2009, the fringe-limbed tree frog was listed as endangered. An epidemic of amphibian chytid fungus spread in Panama which caused the extinction of this frog. Attempts at captive breeding failed. The frogs thrived in captivity, but did not mate.

The last female fringe-limbed tree frog died in 2009. She was survived by 2 males. The health of one of the males failed and he was euthanized on February 17, 2012. The last male was named Toughie. He lived all by himself at the Atlanta Botanical Garden. He died September 26, 2016.

CARSTEN R. JORGENSEN

PART II

ENDANGERED SPECIES

CARSTEN R. JORGENSEN

45 ENDANGERED SPECIES

Extinction is a natural occurrence. The natural rate of extinction is about one or five every year. At this time the extinction rate is approximately 100 extinctions per million. This is 1,000 times higher than the natural rate. It is predicted that future rates could be as much as 10,000 times higher.

Humans are destroying animal species (not just individuals but complete species) at a fantastic rate. Scientists state that we are in the sixth mass extinction event and it is caused by humans. Dozens of species are going extinct every day. The species which are declining include mammals, birds, reptiles, arthropods (insects and arachnids) fish, crustaceans, corals and other cnidarians. In many cases this decline is severe.

Humans use many weapons in their pursuit of species eradication. These weapons include poaching, introduction of non-native species, habitat destruction, exploitation, and climate change.

Insect populations have decreased by more than 75% worldwide over the last 28 years. Eighty percent of plants rely on bees and other insects for pollination. Sixty percent of bird species rely on insects for food.

The extinction of a species leads to extinctions of more species bound to that species in the ecological web. As ecosystems unravel, the number of extinctions will snowball. It has been estimated that by the middle of this century we will have lost 50% of the planet's animal species.

Many thousands of species are at risk of disappearing forever in the coming decades. The following is a description of some of these species.

46 WHALES

A Whale Jumping

The International Whaling Commission (IWC) was formed in 1946 with 89 member governments. Its purpose was to conserve whales and manage whales around the world.

The IWC banned commercial whaling in 1986. Whaling for scientific purposes was exempt. Examples are reproductive studies and food analysis (stomach contents).

Japan took up whaling for scientific purposes to use whales for exploitation. (Japanese people eat whale meat.). In 2016, Japanese whalers killed about 300 whales in the Antarctic including more than 200 pregnant females. Whales were deliberately hunted "by accident".

Japan pursued a well funded campaign to allow commercial whaling. This has been consistently turned down. Instead of accepting the IWC decision, Japan walked out. It left the IWC on December 21, 2018.

Japan is a leading voice among pro-whaling countries, and it is feared that other pro-whaling countries may also walk out. These countries include South Korea and Russia.

Because of its withdrawal from the IWC, Japan can no longer hunt whales under the scam of whaling for scientific purposes in international waters. It is restricted to whaling in Japanese waters. The whales in the Antarctic are a little safer now. Some countries are now imposing sanctions by denying Japan to fish in their waters.

47 TIGERS

Tiger

Tigers are native to Asia. Their range today are much smaller than it used to be. Today they are found in South-east Asia, India, western China, and some parts of Russia. There are breeding populations in Bhutan, Bangladesh, India, Malaysia, Indonesia, Thailand, Russia, and Nepal.

They prefer areas with dense cover, such as forests, with plenty of prey. They also prefer to be near water. Unlike other large cats they like to get into the water to cool off. Dens are in secluded areas such as caves, hollow trees, and among dense vegetation.

Tigers are nocturnal hunters and capable of taking down prey over twice their size.

Tigers are endangered. Three sub-species of tigers have already been wiped out within the last 80 years. That is an average of 1 every 20 years. This is an alarming rate. It has been predicted by some that all tigers may become extinct in the wild within the next decade. Some of the biggest threats are poaching, reduction of prey availability, and loss of habitat due to agriculture and urbanization.

48 AMUR LEOPARD

The Amur Leopard

The Amur leopard is also called the Far East leopard, the Manchurian leopard, and the Korean leopard. Their range is very small. They live in a temperate forest which is crossed by the Amur River, a natural border between Russia and China.

The Amur leopard is the only leopard adapted to survive in extreme snowy weather and hot summer climates. They eat wild pigs, badgers, roe and sika deer, and hares. Occasionally they also eat black bear. If they have left over food, they drag it away and hide it for left over day.

The Amur leopard is on the brink of extinction. Of all the leopards, the Amur leopard is the most critically endangered.

There are less than 90 left in the wild. The main threats are hunting for their fur, habitat loss to agriculture and urban development, hunting of prey species, and human made forest fires.

In 2012 the Russian government established the Land Of The Leopard National Park which is about 647,000 acres of prime leopard habitat where they can live and breed in safety. The park has a network of 400 camera traps placed across 890,000 acres of leopard habitat. Scientists compare the photos taken, looking for each cat's unique fur patterns, to come up with the population counts each year. However, the snow-covered national park already contains about as much prey as it can support, so getting the population to grow much further could be a challenge.

49 BLACK RHINOCEROS

The Black Rhinoceros

In 2018 the Chinese state media reported that 57 traditional medicinal centers were being developed in places including Poland, the United Arab Emirate, and France. Traditional Chinese Medicine is now found in over 180 countries, almost all the world's recognized nations. The industry is worth over $60 billion a year.

To treat or prevent health problems, herbs and animal parts are used. Some conservationists worry that the World Health Organization's decision to support Chinese Traditional Medicine and the growing popularity of Traditional Chinese Medicine may cause extinctions of endangered species historically used for Chinese cures.

Cathy Dean is chief executive officer of Save the Rhinos which is a London-based charity that raises money for rhino conservation. Cathy Dean has stated "It would be totally wrong if respecting the cultural belief of one country, China, led to the extinction of Africa's biological heritage".

Chris Shepherd, executive director of Monitor, a British Columbia organization combating illegal wildlife trade, has stated, "It is no coincidence that the species most sought after with the Traditional Chinese Medicine are the most critically endangered species. There are a number of species that are already threatened or critically endangered by the traditional medicine trade. Any growth in that area or in demand for these species could be devastating."

The species Chris referred to were pangolins, big cats, rhinoceros, and other threatened species.

One of the items sought after for Traditional Chinese Medicine is rhinoceros horns.

The Black Rhinoceros

The black rhinoceros is found in Kenya, Tanzania, Nimibia, South Africa, and Zimbabwe. The population declined by 96% between 1970 and 1992. The black rhinoceros is critically endangered and is at risk from illegal poaching. In 1995 there were only 2,410 individuals left.

A subspecies, the western black rhinoceros is now extinct. The last Javan rhino outside Java is also believed to have disappeared.

As for their cousin, the northern white rhino, as of March 2018, there are only **two** of them left, both of which are female. They live in the Ol Pejeta Conservancy in Kenya and are protected round-the-clock by armed guards. Their near extinction is also due to decades of rampant poaching for rhino horn.

If a Rhino is dehorned without cutting into the skull, it can grow back to almost full size after three years. However, if the rhino's skull is cut into while being dehorned, it could complicate or completely compromise the re-growth of the horn. Unfortunately, poachers shoot to kill and take the horns and leave the rest of the body.

Dehorning is one method used to help to protect the rhinos. Without the prize of a horn, the poachers are not interested. It is not an easy thing to remove the horns of a live rhinoceros. It requires helicopters and dart guns with tranquilizers. The horn is carefully taken off with a chain saw. When done correctly, the removal of the horn does not hurt the animal and is like clipping a toenail. Dehorning has to be done every 18 to 24 months since the horns do grow back. However, conservationists can not remove the horns from just one rhinoceros. They must remove them from all the rhinos in the park because those without horns would be more vulnerable against those with horns in any territorial fights.

A Rhinoceros with its horns removed for its safety

Dehorning does not eliminate the threat of poaching entirely. Trophy hunters prize both the head and the horns so, the threat from hunters still exists. However, this strategy does make a big difference in several reserves since nearly a quarter of rhino deaths occur on private reserves. With the introduction of dehorning, this death rate has dropped by five percent. This is not a solution though and only buys the rhinos some more time.

To help protect the remaining black rhinoceros, a French tech company, Sigfox, has recently developed a small tracker that can be inserted into the horns of rhinos. They have developed sensors that are able to give the exact location of rhinos. The sensors can alert park rangers when rhinos approach an area known to be particularly dangerous due to previous instances of poaching. Combined with other warning sensors, they can be used to get rescue teams to the location the rhinos are at.

50 PANGOLIN

The Pangolin

The pangolin is the only mammal in the world covered with scales. They eat about 70 million insects each year. They are about the size of a small cat. They spend their time up in trees or sleeping in burrows underground.

There are eight species of pangolin. Four are found in Asia. They are the Chinese pangolin, the Malayan pangolin, the Indian pangolin, and the Palawan pangolin. Four are found in Africa: the tree pangolin, the giant ground pangolin, the Cape pangolin, and the long tail pangolin.

They are critically endangered. The cause is poaching. The pangolin scales are used in Traditional Chinese Medicine. The pangolin is the most trafficked animal in the world. It is estimated that a pangolin is stolen from the wild every 5 minutes. The scales can be sold on the black market for up to $3,000.00 per kilogram.

Pangolins are not able to easily be reintroduced into the wild once they have been rescued from illegal trade. Attempts to reproduce pangolins in captivity are also often unsuccessful due to their need for specific food and habitats. Pangolins are very fragile, despite their protective scales. Their immune responses are lower than most animals, and they are susceptible to diseases such as pneumonia and the development of ulcers when in captivity. These things can lead to an early death.

A pangolin in defensive posture, Horniman Museum, London

51 SAOLA

The Saola or Asian Unicorn
Photo: Silviculture - CC BY SA 3.0, GNU Free Documentation License
https://commons.wikimedia.org/wiki/File:Pseudoryx_nghetinhensis,_b.PNG

The saola also called the Asian unicorn was discovered in 1992. Just after its discovery, it was declared critically endangered. Since its discovery, it has been photographed only three times in the wild.

The appearance of the saola is like an antelope. However, its closest genetic cousins are cattle. The scientific classification was so difficult that a new genetic tribe was invented.

The saola are found in only one place in the world. That is the Annamite mountains forest on the border between Vietnam and Laos.

There have been very few saola in captivity. One saola was observed while in captivity in 1996. She was there for 18 days. Then, she died of unknown causes.

Not very much is known about the saola, but they are critically endangered. The main threat is loss of habitat. In the nature reserve area of Bu Huong, commercial logging has been stopped in an effort to protect their habitat. There is now an official ban on forest clearance within the boundaries of the reserve, however, this does not protect the habitat of those that may be living outside of the reserve.

Saola are also illegally hunted by local hunters. The meat is used in restaurants and food markets. Saola is also used for traditional medicines and prized for it's fur. Hunters gain high esteem in the village for bringing home a saola carcass because it is so rare. The people in the villages are traditional hunters, and their attitude about killing the saola is hard to change; this makes conservation difficult.

Saola also sometimes get accidentally caught in snares that have been set to catch other animals, such as wild boar, sambar, and muntjac, that raid local crops. Conservation groups go out and remove the snares from saola habitats on a regular basis. More than 26,000 snares have been removed from these habitats so far.

52 GORILLA

Gorillas

Gorillas are one of our closest living relatives. They share between 95% and 99% of their DNA with humans. There are two different gorilla species. Each of those species has two sub species. The Western gorilla has the Western Lowland gorilla and the Cross River gorilla. The Eastern gorilla has the Mountain gorilla and the Eastern Lowland gorilla.

All the four subspecies are in danger from habitat loss and hunting. Body parts are sold to collectors, and baby gorillas are sold illegally as pets, research subjects, or private zoo animals.

The rarest is the Cross River gorilla. It has fewer than 300 members left. It has eight small isolated populations in Nigeria and Cameroon.

53 ORANGUTAN

Orangutan Mother and Child

Orangutans and humans share 96.4% DNA. Scientists have discovered that orangutans have a sense of empathy and mimicry that forms an essential part of laughter. They are known for their high intelligence and their use of tools. Orangutans in the care of humans have learned sign language. In rescue centers orangutans have done tasks of humans such as washing clothes, hammering nails into wood, and rowing boats.

Orangutan Father

The orangutan is found on the Malaysian islands of Borneo and Sumatra. Its name means 'wild man of the woods'. Its forest habitat is being rapidly destroyed by conversion to agriculture. Most of the lowland forests of Sumatra and Borneo have been cleared and turned into agricultural fields. This has forced them to move into higher elevation forests. These forests are less productive and can not support the same population as the lowland forests.

Another problem for the orangutan is the poachers. The poachers shoot the mother orangutan and take the babies for the pet trade. Baby orangutans are very desirable pets in Asia. A Taiwanese television station featured a baby orangutan as a pet. Then, 2,000 baby orangutans were captured and shipped to Taiwan for the pet trade. It is estimated that 6,000 mothers were killed and 4,000 captured babies died to supply the 2,000 pets.

Baby Orangutans End Up in Rehabilitation Centers

When the baby orangutans grow up, they become difficult pets and the owners ask officials to take them away. These orangutans are no longer capable of living in the wild. They must then live in rehabilitation centers for the rest of their lives. Sumatra and Borneo can not afford these centers so, they are dependent on charitable contributions from conservation groups in other countries.

54 SEA TURTLES

The hawksbill sea turtle swimming over a colony of elkhorn coral

Photo Credit: Caroline Rogers, U.S. Geological Survey. Public domain.

The hawksbill sea turtle lives in the warm coastline waters of the world's oceans from the Atlantic Ocean to the Pacific Ocean and the Indian Ocean. Research suggests there are only five populations in the world with only 1,000 females breeding annually.

The hawksbill turtle is omnivorous. Its main food supply is coral reef sponges. These sponges are poisonous to all other animals so, they have little competition for this resource.

The hawksbill turtle is the most endangered turtle. It is the fourth most endangered species on the planet. Their gold and brown patterned shells are sold on the black market to make ornamental products and valuable jewelry. In Japan the hawksbill turtle shell has been part of the traditional culture for 300 years. It is still used in traditional wedding dresses.

Trade in the hawksbill turtle shell is illegal and it is the most frequent item seized by custom officials.

CARSTEN R. JORGENSEN

55 SUMATRAN ELEPHANT

The Sumatran Elephant

The Sumatran elephant roams in the lowland forests of Sumatra, an island in Indonesia. The biggest threat to this elephant is habitat loss. Between 1980 and 2005, 69% of the Sumatran elephant habitat was lost. The result was that 50% of Sumatran elephants died. The habitat loss came about because the growing human population needed more agricultural land and living space.

The Sumatran elephant is also preyed upon by poachers who are agriculturalists with palm oil plantations. The poaching is done by poisoning, electrocution, and trapping.

The International Union for the Conservation of Nature (IUCN) has declared the Sumatran elephant critically endangered. Organizations have called on the Sumatran Agriculture Ministry to tighten restrictions.

56 VAQUITA

The Vaquita

The vaquita are the most endangered marine animal in the world. There are now only an estimated 12 left in existence. Their survival is threatened by the fishing industry, pollution, and the dam built in the Colorado River.

The vaquita are also known as cochito, vaquita marina, and Gulf of California harbour porpoise. They are found in only one place which is the narrow body of water lying between the peninsula of Baia California and the North west coast of mainland Mexico.

Vaquitas are compared to porpoises and often confused with dolphins. The vaquitas are smaller and have no snout. Their bodies are also chunkier. They are the smallest cetaceans in the world and are cousins with the largest animal in the world, the blue whale.

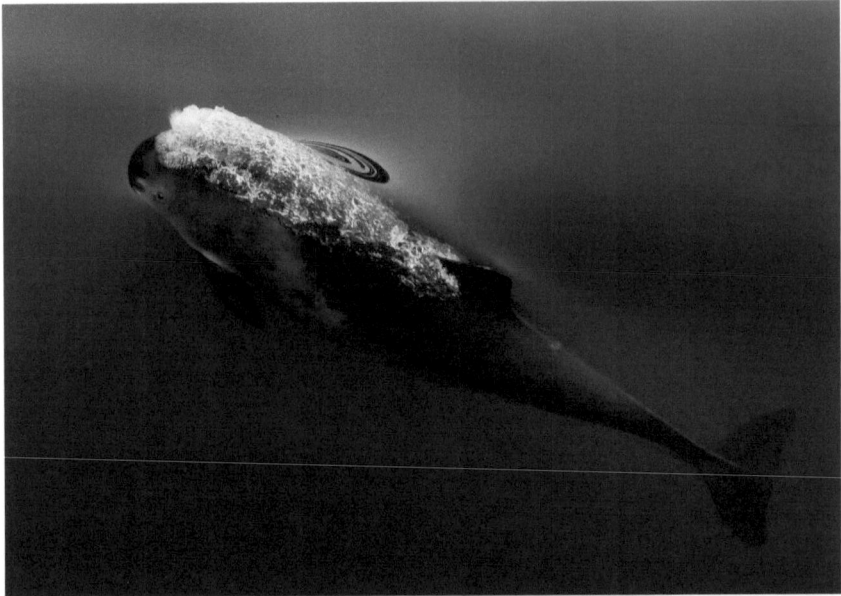

Gill nets are the biggest threat to the vaquitas. The complete elimination of gillnet fishing in the range of the vaquita has been identified as the key element necessary for the survival of the species. In an effort to save the vaquita, the Mexican government banned the use of gill nets in 2015. A long-term Vaquita Refuge Area was also established where all commercial fishing is banned. Despite these efforts, the population of vaquita continue to decline due to illegal gill netting. The illegal gill nets are set by poachers to catch the totoaba fish, which are also critically endangered, and the vaquita are not the intended target. However, the vaquita are the victims of the gill nets just the same. At the current rate of loss, the vaquita will likely decline to extinction in the next few years unless complete elimination of gillnet fishing is achieved and effectively enforced. It has become obvious that illegal gill net fishing can not be completely eradicated and so last ditch efforts were attempted.

A conservation group called "VaquitaCPR", in conjunction with various government bodies, had put a plan into motion to try to help save the vaquitas. The plan was going to be implemented in multiple phases.

Phase one: Locating, Catching, Initial Housing, & Animal Care
Phase two: Sanctuary Housing and Care
Phase three: Long Term Sanctuary Housing
Phase four: Reintroduction to the Gulf of California

Greater details about this plan can be found on their website : https://www.vaquitacpr.org/vaquitacpr-conservation-program-plan/

Unfortunately, shortly after this plan was set in motion, it had to be shut down. The first vaquita caught was so stressed out that they had to release it. They attempted a capture a second time and that resulted in the death of a breeding-age female vaquita. It was decided that they could not risk losing another vaquita so, they gave up this plan. All they can do now is send ships out to find and remove as many gill nets as they can. The future of the vaquita is very bleak.

Every effort to save them takes a great deal of money, support, and research. Help is needed through donations as well as making other people aware of the situation. To find out more about how to help, visit the vaquita CPR website:

https://www.vaquitacpr.org

or the Porpoise Conservation Society website :

https://porpoise.org

where you can help by adopting a vaquita, sign a petition, report sightings, volunteer, and support conservation efforts.

57 TOTOABA

A totoaba with a vaquita caught in the net as a bycatch
NOAA Fisheries picture from 1992 , photo by Omar Vidal

The totoaba is the largest member of the drum family. It can grow to over 6 feet in length and reach a weight of 220 pounds. It eats finned fish and crustaceans. It is found only in the Gulf of California in Mexico. It is critically endangered.

There was a commercial fishery for totoaba which drove down its population. In 1975, Mexico put a ban on fishing for totoaba.

The vaquita, the world's rarest marine mammal, has been almost eradicated by pirate fishermen catching the totoaba and killing the vaquita. The vaquita drown in gill nets set for totoaba. The totoaba is caught for its swim bladder because of Chinese traditional medicine. The swim bladders are smuggled to China where they are sold on the black market for up to $20,000.00 per kilogram.

58 GOLDEN-HEADED LANGUR

The Golden-Headed Langur
By Zhijin Liu, Christian Roos, Boshi Wang, et al , CC BY, 2013
www.ncbi.nlm.nih.gov/pmc/articles/PMC3629164/figure/pone-0061659-g001/

The golden-headed langur, also known as the Cat Ba langur, lives in northern Vietnam on Cat Ba Island in forests containing limestone hills. It reaches a head to body length of almost two feet and a weight of 44 pounds. They are diurnal and arboreal. They sleep in caves. One langur group may have up to 12 different resting caves. The main food of the langur is leaves. But sometimes they eat fresh shoots, flowers, bark, and some fruit which are poisonous to humans.

The golden headed langur is critically endangered due to habitat destruction and illegal poaching and trapping for traditional medicinal purposes by local people and from poachers outside the Island who are part of the international illegal wildlife trade. There is now a strictly protected sanctuary on the eastern coast of Cat Ba Island, in a National Park and it supports about 40% of the population. Rangers have been hired as bodyguards to protect the population and their environment, but this is a dangerous job.

Since the beginning of the conservation efforts, nine langurs have been born and only three have died of natural causes.

Golden-Headed Langur Babies

There are less than 70 golden-headed langur left. They live in 5 groups across the island and only three of those groups are breeding. There is hope for them since their population is up from only 40 individuals in 2003. But it is a very slow process.

59 HORNED MARSUPIAL FROG

The Horned Marsupial Frog
By Brian Gratwicke , CC BY- 4.0,
https://www.inaturalist.org/taxa/64737-Hemiphractidae

The horned marsupial frog is native to Columbia, Ecuador, and eastern Panama where it lives high in the canopy of rain forests.

After a female horned marsupial frog lays eggs, the male fertilizes them and very carefully places them in a pouch on the female's back. There her babies incubate and feed off nutrients in the eggs and grow. The young hatch in the pouch, not as tadpoles but as fully formed tiny frogs.

The horned marsupial frog was thought to be extinct in 2005.

A team of biologists from the conservation and eco-tour group, Tropical Herping, were exploring a remote part of the Choco region in western Ecuador when they heard frog calls they did not recognize. They searched with flashlights. Team member Sebastian Di Dominico said, "When we finally spied the noise-maker and saw that it was the horned marsupial frog, we were so excited we started to jump up and down.

The team found the horned marsupial frog in 2018. The find suggested a healthy stable population in a rare patch of healthy forest just outside the Cotacatchi – Cayapas Ecological Reserve. They were able to collect four frogs including a pregnant female.

The efforts of the Panama Amphibian Rescue and Conservation Project, scientists at the Botanical Garden in the United States, El Valle Amphibian Conservation Center of Panama, and the Summit Zoo of Panama, were successful in the breeding of horned marsupial frogs. It looks as if this species will be brought back from near extinction.

60 GIRAFFES

The West African Giraffe

It is not widely known that the giraffe has recently made the list of endangered species. There are four main species (the Masai, Northern, Southern, and Reticulated) and nine subspecies of giraffe. Two of these subspecies are now critically endangered; the Nubian giraffe and the Kordofan giraffe (both are subspecies of the Northern giraffe). All four giraffe species and their subspecies live in geographically distinct areas throughout Africa.

West African giraffes (also a subspecies of the Northern giraffe) is the smallest subspecies. They have grown from 50 individuals in the 1990s to about 600 today. Its last self-sustaining herd is in southwest Niger. Although the West African giraffes have a small population, their numbers are rising so, they are now listed as "vulnerable".

The Reticulated Giraffe is now listed as endangered

Other species are declining in population and are now endangered, such as the Reticulated giraffe.

Giraffes appear to select mates of the same coat pattern type, which are imprinted on them as calves. So, the four main categories of giraffe (the Masai, Northern, Southern, and Reticulated) do not inter-breed with each other. Just like human fingerprints, no two giraffe have the same coat pattern.

The giraffes face two main threats, encroachment from cities and towns into their habitat and poaching. Many giraffes are slaughtered just for their tails, which are considered a status symbol and have been used as a dowry when asking a bride's father for his daughters hand in marriage in some cultures. Others are killed for their skins which are used to make luxury items. Sometimes, they are also killed for their meat which is enough to feed families for weeks. It doesn't help that in some populations, over 50% of all giraffe calves do not survive their first year. And sadly, giraffe outside protected areas are sometimes also struck by vehicles and trains.

"There's a strong tendency to think that familiar species (such as giraffes, chimps, etc.) must be OK because they are familiar and we see them in zoos," - Duke University conservation biologist Stuart Pimm

The Nubian Giraffe is listed as critically endangered

The Nubian giraffe used to be widespread everywhere on Northeast Africa. Now it is only found in Ethiopia, Kenya, Uganda, South Sudan and Sudan. Their population sits at only 3000 in the wild.

The Kordofan Giraffe is listed as critically endangered

Compared to the other subspecies, the Kordofan giraffe is relatively small at 5 to 6 meters. Their population sits at only 2000 in the wild. They are found in northern Cameroon, southern Chad, Central African Republic, and possibly western Sudan.

If you add up the subspecies of the Northern giraffe (West African 600, Nubian 3000, and Kordofan 2000) there is only a total of 5600 ranging from Niger to Ethiopia. Giraffes are already extinct in at least seven countries in Africa.

61 MONARCH BUTTERFLY

The Monarch Butterfly male

The Monarch Butterfly female

Each year the monarch butterfly migrates from the northern United States and Canada to overwinter in California and Mexico. In 2018, the number of western monarch butterflies overwintering in California had dropped to 20,456 butterflies. This was a drop of 86 % since the year before. The number of eastern monarch butterflies overwintering in Mexico had dropped 15 % since the year before which was a total decline of over 80 % over the last 20 years. Humans are responsible.

Humans are causing habitat loss of the monarch butterfly. Humans are destroying milkweed which is the only food monarch caterpillars will eat. Some scientists also think that the increased carbon dioxide in the air may be making milkweed too toxic for the monarch caterpillars to eat.

You can help the monarch butterfly by planting milkweed, creating a monarch-friendly habitat, and not using pesticides.

62 SCHAUS SWALLOWTAIL BUTTERFLY

The Schaus Swallowtail Butterfly
Photo by Susan Kolterman /U.S. Fish and Wildlife Service

The Schaus swallowtail butterfly is found only in Biscayne National Park and on northern Key Largo, a single island in Florida.

These butterflies have been attacked by the use of insecticide, habitat destruction, droughts, hurricanes, and illegal collections. The Schaus swallowtail butterfly was declared endangered in 1984. Biological technicians count the Schaus swallowtails at Biscayne National Park near Miami each year. In 2011, they counted 41 butterflies. In 2012, there were only five.

An emergency authorization allows the University of Florida to catch up to 4 female Schaus swallowtails. These prisoners are confined in mesh cages. Each day the eggs they lay are removed for incubation. After four days, the female swallowtails are released. The swallowtails hatched from the eggs are released in their natural habitat in Biscayne National Park.

It is estimated that there is now a few hundred of them on northern Key Largo and more are being released each year.

Content:

63 CONCLUSION

Scientists have estimated that about 20,000 species are near extinction. The International Union for Conservation of Natures Red List of Threatened Species has a global inventory of species. They are learning more about where species are through modern technology. Scientists studying the problem suspect that if things keep going the way they are, extinction rates will increase which will result in the Sixth Mass Extinction. The animals presented in this book is only a small sample of the events happening.

The rate of extinctions is 100 to 1,000 species per million per year. It has been found that before humans arrived, the rate of extinction was 1 per million per year. The main cause is habitat destruction by humans and climate change. Many species are unable to adapt to the changes human are inflicting on the Earth, and are facing extinction. In fact, predictions estimate that up to 1 million species may become extinct as a result of climate change.

The World Health Organization (WHO) is encouraging the Chinese Traditional Medicine (CTM). The logic is that modern medicine is too expensive. However, expanding the CTM is a danger for the world's threatened species such as the black rhinoceros, and the totoaba. Some medicine outlets carry dried frogs, deer penis, boxes of Tibetan caterpillar fungus. Not all the CTM deal in animal parts. CTM also uses herbal medicine and acupuncture. However, a large part is alarming such as the swim bladders of totoaba, scales of the pangolin, and black rhinoceros horns.

A species does not exist in isolation. It is part of the web of life. In the Walt Disney movie 'The Lion King' it is called the 'Circle of Life'. This web of life, or the planet's ecology, supports the life on planet earth. Extinctions can lead to more extinctions because of the interdependence of one species on others. Thus, extinctions could have a domino effect of extinctions. We humans could become endangered with continued extinctions.

People can be active and prevent these extinctions. They can vote for policies that lessen the effects of climate change. People can also encourage their governments to connect one nature reserve to another. People can also band together on the local level to protect rare or endangered species.

CARSTEN R. JORGENSEN

REFERENCES

"Toward an Interactive Theory of Nature and Culture: Ecology, Production, and Cognition in the California Fishing Industry." Arthur F. McEvoy.

"The Ends Of The Earth: Perspectives on Modern Environmental History". edited by Donald Worster. Cambridge University Press, 1988. New York, USA., Pg 211

Becky Chung, (May 30, 2013) "10 fascinating facts about woolly mammoths"
Retreived from
https://blog.ted.com/10-fascinating-facts-about-woolly-mammoths/

Wikipedia contributors. "Irish elk." *Wikipedia, The Free Encyclopedia*. Wikipedia, The Free Encyclopedia, 26 Mar. 2019. Web. 30 Mar. 2019.
Retreived from
https://en.wikipedia.org/w/index.php?title=Special:CiteThisPage&page=Irish_elk&id=889586383

Wikipedia contributors. "Quagga." *Wikipedia, The Free Encyclopedia*. Wikipedia, The Free Encyclopedia, 30 Mar. 2019. Web. 30 Mar. 2019.
Retreived from
https://en.wikipedia.org/wiki/Quagga

Wikipedia contributors. "Atlas bear." *Wikipedia, The Free Encyclopedia*. Wikipedia, The Free Encyclopedia, 5 Dec. 2018. Web. 30 Mar. 2019.
Retreived from
https://en.wikipedia.org/wiki/Atlas_bear

Wikipedia contributors. "Golden toad." *Wikipedia, The Free Encyclopedia*. Wikipedia, The Free Encyclopedia, 16 Feb. 2019. Web. 30 Mar. 2019.
Retreived from
https://en.wikipedia.org/wiki/Golden_toad

Andrew Curry (March 1, 2010) "Global warming didn't Kill The Golden Toad"
Retreived from
https://www.sciencemag.org/news/2010/03/global-warming-didnt-kill-golden-toad

Savage, J., Pounds, J. & Bolaños, F. 2008. *Incilius periglenes. The IUCN Red List of Threatened Species* 2008: e.T3172A9654595.
Retreived from
https://www.iucnredlist.org/species/3172/9654595

Katharine Corriveau, "Specimen Spotlight -- Passenger Pigeon (*Ectopistes migratorius*)"
Retreived from
http://mvz.berkeley.edu/Newsletter/newsletter_files/201408/Passenger_Pigeon.php

Madhava Meegaskumbura, Kelum Manamendra-Arachchi, Christopher J. Schneider, Rohan Pethiyagoda ,Vol 1397, No 1 > "New species amongst Sri Lanka's extinct shrub frogs (Amphibia: Rhacophoridae: Philautus)"
Retreived from
https://biotaxa.org/Zootaxa/article/view/zootaxa.1397.1.1

Wikipedia contributors. "Sea mink." *Wikipedia, The Free Encyclopedia*. Wikipedia, The Free Encyclopedia, 11 Mar. 2019. Web. 30 Mar. 2019.
Retreived from
https://en.wikipedia.org/wiki/sea_mink

Loren Posey, "Sea Mink: Facts & Extinction"
Retreived from
https://study.com/academy/lesson/sea-mink-facts-extinction.html

Peter Maas.nl (2018) "Globally Extinct Amphibians"
Retreived from
https://petermaas.nl/extinct/lists/globally-extinct-amphibians/

Ben Crair (May 2018) "Why did the Carolina Parakeet go extinct?"
Retreived from
https://www.smithsonianmag.com/science-nature/why-carolina-parakeet-go-extinct-180968740/

Wikipedia contributors. "Bubal hartebeest." *Wikipedia, The Free Encyclopedia*. Wikipedia, The Free Encyclopedia, 2 Feb. 2019. Web. 30 Mar. 2019
Retreived from
https://en.wikipedia.org/wiki/Bubal_hartebeest

Wikipedia contributors. "Gravenche." *Wikipedia, The Free Encyclopedia.* Wikipedia, The Free Encyclopedia, 1 Jul. 2018. Web. 30 Mar. 2019.
Retreived from
https://en.wikipedia.org/wiki/Gravenche

Wikipedia contributors. "Saddle-backed Rodrigues giant tortoise." *Wikipedia, The Free Encyclopedia.* Wikipedia, The Free Encyclopedia, 31 May. 2018. Web. 30 Mar. 2019.
Retreived from
https://en.wikipedia.org/wiki/Saddle-backed_Rodrigues_giant_tortoise

Wikipedia contributors. "Domed Rodrigues giant tortoise." *Wikipedia, The Free Encyclopedia.* Wikipedia, The Free Encyclopedia, 6 Oct. 2018. Web. 30 Mar. 2019.
Retreived from
https://en.wikipedia.org/wiki/Domed_Rodrigues_giant_tortoise

Bryan Nelson (May 6, 2011) "13 animals hunted to extinction"
Retreived from
https://www.mnn.com/earth-matters/animals/photos/13-animals-hunted-to-extinction/toolache-wallaby

Department of the Environment (2019). "*Notamacropus greyi* in Species Profile and Threats Database, Department of the Environment, Canberra."
Retreived from
http://www.environment.gov.au/cgi-bin/sprat/public/publicspecies.pl?taxon_id=232

Wikipedia contributors. "Yunnan lake newt." *Wikipedia, The Free Encyclopedia*. Wikipedia, The Free Encyclopedia, 28 Mar. 2019. Web. 30 Mar. 2019.
Retreived from
https://en.wikipedia.org/wiki/Yunnan_lake_newt

Wikipedia contributors. "Caribbean monk seal." *Wikipedia, The Free Encyclopedia*. Wikipedia, The Free Encyclopedia, 24 Jan. 2019. Web. 30 Mar. 2019.
Retreived from
https://en.wikipedia.org/wiki/Caribbean_monk_seal

Wikipedia contributors. "Thicktail chub." *Wikipedia, The Free Encyclopedia*. Wikipedia, The Free Encyclopedia, 29 Jan. 2019. Web. 30 Mar. 2019
Retreived from
https://en.wikipedia.org/wiki/Thicktail_chub

Wikipedia contributors. "Tecopa pupfish." *Wikipedia, The Free Encyclopedia*. Wikipedia, The Free Encyclopedia, 8 Aug. 2018. Web. 30 Mar. 2019.
Retreived from
https://en.wikipedia.org/wiki/Tecopa_pupfish

Wikipedia contributors. "Galapagos damsel." *Wikipedia, The Free Encyclopedia*. Wikipedia, The Free Encyclopedia, 16 Feb. 2019. Web. 30 Mar. 2019.
Retreived from
https://en.wikipedia.org/wiki/Galapagos_damsel

Wayne Schaefer and Steve Schaefer (March 5, 2015) "Journal Article, 2015"
Retreived from
http://wayneschaefer.blogspot.com/

Wikipedia contributors. "Blue walleye." *Wikipedia, The Free Encyclopedia*. Wikipedia, The Free Encyclopedia, 12 Nov. 2018. Web. 30 Mar. 2019
Retreived from
https://en.wikipedia.org/wiki/Blue_walleye

Gary of Walleye Heaven, "Blue Walleye"
Retreived from
https://www.walleyeheaven.com/blue-walleye.htm

"Biology and Culture of Percid Fishes: Principles and Practices" edited by Patrick Kestemont, Konrad Dabrowski, Robert C. Summerfelt , pg 21

Wikipedia contributors. "Gastric-brooding frog." *Wikipedia, The Free Encyclopedia*. Wikipedia, The Free Encyclopedia, 4 Feb. 2019. Web. 30 Mar. 2019
Retreived from
https://en.wikipedia.org/wiki/Gastric-brooding_frog

Wikipedia contributors. "Thylacine." *Wikipedia, The Free Encyclopedia*. Wikipedia, The Free Encyclopedia, 30 Mar. 2019. Web. 30 Mar. 2019.
Retreived from
https://en.wikipedia.org/wiki/Thylacine

Wikipedia contributors. "Silver trout." *Wikipedia, The Free Encyclopedia*. Wikipedia, The Free Encyclopedia, 6 Feb. 2019. Web. 30 Mar. 2019.
Retreived from
https://en.wikipedia.org/wiki/Silver_trout

Esther Inglis-Arkell (November 13, 2015) "An extinct giant gecko was found stuffed in a museum basement"
Retreived from
https://gizmodo.com/this-specimen-of-an-extinct-giant-gecko-was-found-in-a-1742435773

Aaron M. Bauer & Anthony P. Russell (1986) Hoplodactylusdelcourti n. sp. (Reptilia: Gekkonidae), the largest known gecko, New Zealand Journal of Zoology, 13:1, 141-148, DOI: 10.1080/03014223.1986.10422655
Retreived from
https://doi.org/10.1080/03014223.1986.10422655

Threatened Species Section (2019). Hypolimnus pedderensis *(Lake Pedder Earthworm): Species Management Profile for Tasmania's Threatened Species* Department of Primary Industries, Parks, Water and Environment, Tasmania. Accessed on 30/1/2019.
Retreived from
https://www.threatenedspecieslink.tas.gov.au/Pages/Lake-Pedder-Earthworm.aspx

Wikipedia contributors. "Xerces blue." *Wikipedia, The Free Encyclopedia*. Wikipedia, The Free Encyclopedia, 6 Feb. 2019. Web. 31 Mar. 2019.
Retreived from
https://en.wikipedia.org/wiki/Xerces_blue

Geoff Read (April 2007) "Re-description of the Lake Pedder Earthworm: Hypolimnus pedderensis – the first extinct earthworm listed on IUCN Red List of the World's Threatened Spp."
Retreived from
http://www.annelida.net/earthworm/Tasmanian %20Earthworms/Hpedderensis.pdf

Tasmania Department of Primary Industries, Parks, Water and Environment (December 11, 2017) "Cascade Funnel-Web Spider"
Retreived from
https://dpipwe.tas.gov.au/conservation/threatened-species-and-communities/lists-of-threatened-species/threatened-species-invertebrates/threatened-species-invertebrate-animals-e-z/cascade-funnel-web-spider

Mark Hoddle (2013) "A Critical Analysis of the Extinction of *Levuana iridescens* in Fiji by *Bessa remota*"
Retreived from
https://biocontrol.ucr.edu/hoddle/levuana.html

Wikipedia contributors. "Madeiran large white." *Wikipedia, The Free Encyclopedia*. Wikipedia, The Free Encyclopedia, 30 Mar. 2018. Web. 31 Mar. 2019.
Retreived from
https://en.wikipedia.org/wiki/Madeiran_large_white

Wikipedia contributors. "Ecnomiohyla rabborum." *Wikipedia, The Free Encyclopedia*. Wikipedia, The Free Encyclopedia, 15 Mar. 2019. Web. 31 Mar. 2019
Retreived from
https://en.wikipedia.org/wiki/Ecnomiohyla_rabborum

Franco Andreone & Elena Gavetti (1998) Some remarkable specimens of the giant cape verde skink, macroscincuscoctei (Duméril & Bibron, 1839), with notes about its distribution and causes of its possible extinction, Italian Journal of Zoology, 65:4, 413-421, DOI: 10.1080/11250009809386783
Retreived from
https://doi.org/10.1080/11250009809386783

Wikipedia contributors. "Round Island burrowing boa." *Wikipedia, The Free Encyclopedia*. Wikipedia, The Free Encyclopedia, 5 Oct. 2018. Web. 31 Mar. 2019.
Retreived from
https://en.wikipedia.org/wiki/Round_Island_burrowing_boa

Wikipedia contributors. "Pyrenean ibex." *Wikipedia, The Free Encyclopedia*. Wikipedia, The Free Encyclopedia, 25 Mar. 2019. Web. 31 Mar. 2019.
Retreived from
https://en.wikipedia.org/wiki/Pyrenean_ibex

Save The Rhino (November 7, 2013) "Western Black Rhinoceros declared extinct in 2011 – journalists reporting news two years later"
Retreived from
https://www.savetherhino.org/rhino-species/black-rhino/western-black-rhino-declared-extinct-in-2011-journalists-reporting-news-two-years-later/

Wikipedia contributors. "Heath hen." *Wikipedia, The Free Encyclopedia*. Wikipedia, The Free Encyclopedia, 18 Feb. 2019. Web. 31 Mar. 2019.
Retreived from
https://en.wikipedia.org/wiki/Heath_hen

Bob Strauss (March 30, 2017) "Caspian Tiger"
Retreived from
https://www.thoughtco.com/caspian-tiger-1093063

Harvey Day (July 29, 2014) "Eight unfortunate facts about the extinct Caspian tiger"
Retreived from
https://www.independent.co.uk/voices/iv-drip/eight-unfortunate-facts-about-the-extinct-caspian-tiger-9635347.html

Craig Kasnoff (2019) "Tigers in crisis"
Retreived from
http://www.tigersincrisis.com/the_status.htm

World Wildlife Federation (2019) "Amur Leopard"
Retreived from
https://www.worldwildlife.org/species/amur-leopard

Danielle Dufault - Animalogic (June 20, 2017)YouTube Video "Pangolins are the Cutest Animals You've Never Heard Of"
Retreived from
https://www.youtube.com/watch?v=QY1qqZiaTU8&feature=youtu.be

Wikipedia contributors. "Saola." *Wikipedia, The Free Encyclopedia.* Wikipedia, The Free Encyclopedia, 28 Mar. 2019. Web. 31 Mar. 2019.
Retreived from
https://en.wikipedia.org/wiki/Saola
P.A. Smith (August 24, 2014) "Mountain Gorilla"
Retreived from
https://animalfactguide.com/animal-facts/mountain-gorilla/

Wikipedia contributors. "Hawksbill sea turtle." *Wikipedia, The Free Encyclopedia.* Wikipedia, The Free Encyclopedia, 28 Mar. 2019. Web. 31 Mar. 2019.
Retreived from
https://en.wikipedia.org/wiki/Hawksbill_sea_turtle

Phys.org (January 17, 2018)"Critically endangered Sumatran elephant gives birth in Indonesia"
Retreived from
https://phys.org/news/2018-01-critically-endangered-sumatran-elephant-birth.html

About Animals.com(2018) "Sumatran Elephant: Magnificent Creature of Sumatran Island"
Retreived from
https://www.aboutanimals.com/mammal/sumatran-elephant/

Mike Garowecki (November 6, 2017) "Breeding-age female vaquita dies after being taken into captivity"
Retreived from
https://news.mongabay.com/2017/11/breeding-age-female-vaquita-dies-after-being-taken-into-captivity/

Erik Hoffner (March 8, 2018) "Only 12 vaquita porpoises remain, watchdog group reports"
Retreived from
https://news.mongabay.com/2018/03/only-12-vaquita-porpoises-remain-watchdog-groups-report/

Samiksha Jaiswal (April 13, 2018) "White-headed Langur"
Retreived from
https://alchetron.com/White-headed-langur

Josh Davis (March 12, 2018) "There Are Now Only An Estimated 12 Vaquita Left In Existence, Pushing It Ever Closer To Extinction"
Retreived from
https://www.iflscience.com/plants-and-animals/there-are-now-only-an-estimated-12-vaquita-left-in-existence-pushing-it-ever-closer-to-extinction/

John C. Cannon (May 1, 2018) "More than 800 totoaba swim bladders confiscated by Mexican authorities in smuggling busts"
Retreived from
https://news.mongabay.com/2018/05/more-than-800-totoaba-swim-bladders-confiscated-by-mexican-authorities-in-smuggling-busts/

Wikipedia contributors. "Cát Bà Island." *Wikipedia, The Free Encyclopedia*. Wikipedia, The Free Encyclopedia, 18 Mar. 2019. Web. 30 Mar. 2019.
Retreived from
https://en.wikipedia.org/wiki/C%C3%A1t_B%C3%A0_Island#The_Cat_Ba_Langur

Zhijin Liu, Boshi Wang, Tilo Nadler, Guangjian Liu, Tao Sun, Chengming Huang, Qihai Zhou, Jiang Zhou, Tengcheng Que, Ziming Wang, Christian Roos, Ming Li PLoS One. 2013; 8(4): e61659. Published online 2013 Apr 17. doi: 10.1371/journal.pone.0061659 PMCID: PMC3629164 "Relatively Recent Evolution of Pelage Coloration in Colobinae: Phylogeny and Phylogeography of Three Closely Related Langur Species"
Retreived from
https://www.ncbi.nlm.nih.gov/pmc/articles/PMC3629164/

Jennifer S. Holland (December 12, 2018) "Once thought extinct, bizarre horned frog reappears in Ecuador"
Retreived from
https://www.nationalgeographic.com/animals/2018/12/lost-marsupial-frog-rediscovered-ecuador-choco-forest/

Giraffe Conservation Foundation in Action, Research (November 14, 2018) "IUCN Red List Update: *Even though conservation efforts benefit some giraffe, others are in serious trouble...*"
Retreived from
https://giraffeconservation.org/2018/11/14/giraffe-subspecies-update/

Carrie Arnold (December 21, 2018) "We're losing Monarchs fast- here's why"
Retreived from
https://www.nationalgeographic.com/animals/2018/12/monarch-butterflies-risk-extinction-climate-change/

Learn About Nature (2019) "The vanishing Monarch butterflies"
Retreived from
https://www.monarch-butterfly.com/vanishing-monarch-butterflies.html

U.S. Fish & Wildlife Service (December 11, 2015) "Schaus' Swallowtail Butterfly"
Retreived from
https://www.fws.gov/refuge/Crocodile_Lake/wildlife_and_habitat/schaus_swallowtail/

David Goodhue (July 23, 2018) "Six years ago, about four of these butterflies existed. This is how science saved them." Retreived from https://www.miamiherald.com/news/local/community/florida -keys/article215330270.html

ABOUT THE AUTHOR

Carsten Jorgensen dedicated thirty years in studying and managing fisheries for the Ontario Ministry of Natural Resources.

Upon graduation from Queen's University in Kingston, Ontario in 1966, he accepted a biologist position on Lake Temagami with the Ontario Department of Lands and Forests.

In 1968 he also started work on Lake Nipissing. In 1970, Mr. Jorgensen was working full time as the Lake Nipissing Fisheries Assessment Unit Biologist.

In 1970 he married Brenda Black, daughter of Ontario Conservation Officer, Gordon Black.

In 1996 he retired and now enjoys spending his time playing chess, playing darts, doing Tai Chi, and writing books.

OTHER TITLES BY CARSTEN R. JORGENSEN

If you enjoyed this book by Carsten R. Jorgensen, you may also enjoy these other books that he has written:

The Saga Kings -
ISBN-13: 978-09949338-0-5

Trying To Work For The M.N.R. -
ISBN-13: 978-0-9949338-1-2

My World War Two Adventures In Denmark -
ISBN-13: 978-0-9949338-2-9

One School, Two School, Old School, New School -
ISBN-13: 978-0-9949338-3-6

Fishes Of Lake Nipissing -
ISBN-13: 978-0-9949338-4-3

Dragons Of The World And Where They Roam -
ISBN-13: 978-0-9949338-5-0

Myths, Mythology, and Faith -
ISBN-13: 978-0-9949338-6-7

Or check out his author profile on Good Reads for any new and upcoming books he may be working on:

www.goodreads.com/author/show/14680643.Carsten_R_Jorgensen

www.ingramcontent.com/pod-product-compliance
Lightning Source LLC
Chambersburg PA
CBHW040129270326
41928CB00001B/2